50 NOTABLE NEW JERSEY ATHLETES

By:

Michael J. Pellowski

First Edition

1 2 3 4 5   12 11 10 09 08

Cover designed by Desiree Rappa
Interior designed by EnForm Graphic Productions, Inc.
Cover Photos courtesy of The New York Yankees, Los Angeles Dodgers and Indianapolis Colts Football

DEDICATION

To my partner in life and the person whose assistance made this book possible—Judy Snyder Pellowski

SPECIAL THANKS AND SINCERE APPRECIATION TO THE FOLLOWING ORGANIZATIONS, COLLEGES, SPORTS CLUBS, UNIVERSITIES, AND SPORTS MEDIA SERVICES WHOSE COOPERATION AND GENEROSITY MADE THIS BOOK POSSIBLE.

New York Yankees, Ariele Goldman, the Los Angeles Dodgers, Amy Summers, the Dallas Cowboys Football Club, Jancy Briles, the Indianapolis Colts, Pam Humphrey, the Kansas City Chiefs, Josh Looney, NBA Entertainment and Player Marketing, Alex Tarshis, Sacramento Kings Basketball, Devin Blankenship, USA Basketball, Minnesota Vikings Football, Cameron Aisenbrey, Seattle SuperSonics and Storm, Ryan Williams, Carolina Panthers Football, Deedee Mills, Detroit Lions Football, Deanna Caldwell, Rocky Widner NBAE/Getty Images, Yogi Berra Museum and Learning Center, David Kaplan, Rutgers Sports Media, Rutgers Sports Information, Rutgers Athletic Communications, Kevin McConnell, John Wooding, Stacey Brann, Jason Baum, Chris Masters, Larry Levanti, Jim O'Connor, Patti Banks, C. Vivian Stringer—Rutgers Women's Basketball Coach, Greg Schiano—Rutgers Football Coach, Seton Hall University Sports Information and Sports Media, Joe Montefusco, Matt Sweeney, S.R. Smith, Lehigh University Athletics, Mike Stagnitta, Montclair State University Sports Information, Michael Scala, Florida A & M University Athletics and Sports Information, Ronnie Johnson, University of Notre Dame Sports Information, Carol Copley, Syracuse University Athletics and Sports Information, Susan Cornelius Edson, Lake Superior State University, Linda Bouvet, Morehead State Athletic Media Relations, Randy Stacy, University of Iowa Athletics and Sports Media, Theresa J. Walenta, Fordham University Athletics and Sports Information, Joe DiBari, Hall-of-Famer Yogi Berra, NBA Commissioner David Stern, Bruce Baumgartner, College of the Holy Cross- Charles Bare, Matthew J. Pellowski, Martin J. Pellowski, Melanie J. Pellowski, Lisa Myers, and Morgan J. Pellowski.

CONTENTS

FOREWORD

New Jersey has produced and been the home of so many great athletes and famous sports figures it is almost impossible to devise a foolproof method of selecting a mere fifty to profile. All of the sport celebrities profiled have made significant and enduring contributions to the world of sport. Many were born in New Jersey. Others adopted New Jersey as their home and established roots in the Garden State.

The fifty athletes profiled appear in alphabetical order. There is no rank of importance attached to where each one appears in the book.

An honor roll of additional, notable New Jersey athletes and sports figures appears after the conclusion of the profiles. These individuals are equally worthy of being profiled, but space limitations prevented their inclusion in this edition.

INTRODUCTION

Forget all the jokes you've ever heard about New Jersey. There is nothing funny about the Garden State's monumental contributions to the world of sport. However, there is a single exception to that bold statement. Baseball's immortal comedy routine "Who's on First" performed by the famous comedy team of Abbott and Costello has definite roots in New Jersey. Bud Abbott was a native of Asbury Park, New Jersey and Lou Costello was born in Paterson, New Jersey.

In a way, the game of baseball itself also had a New Jersey birth. The first diamond contest using modern baseball rules was played on Elysian Field in Hoboken, New Jersey, on June 19, 1846.

Over the years, the Garden State has had many banner baseball moments.

Before he became the New York Yankees' Iron Horse, Lou Gehrig was scouted playing first base for Columbia University against the Rutgers baseball squad in New Jersey.

Jackie Robinson played his first professional game as a member of the Brooklyn Dodgers organization at Roosevelt Stadium in Jersey City, New Jersey, in 1946.

Abe Manley and his wife, Effa, were the co-owners of the Newark Eagles—the team that won the Negro League World Series in 1946. In 2006, Effa Manley became the first woman ever elected to the Baseball Hall of Fame.

Another New Jersey lady who made her mark in baseball in the 1940s was North Plainfield's Kay "Swish" Blumetta. Kay Blumetta was a star pitcher for the Fort Wayne Daisies in the All-American Girls Professional Baseball League.

New Jersey soil is fertile ground when it comes to athletics. The game of college football sprouted in New Brunswick, New Jersey, on November 6, 1869. On that historic date, athletes from Princeton University faced off against opponents from Rutgers, The State University of New Jersey in college football's inaugural gridiron clash. Rutgers won the contest six goals to four. The two schools began an athletic tradition that spread across the country and has endured for over 135 years.

Amos Alonzo Stagg, one of football's greatest coaches and innovators, was a Jersey guy. Stagg was born in West Orange, New Jersey. He went to Yale and was picked as a member of the first All-America team ever selected (1889). Amos Alonzo Stagg invented football's onside kick and man-in-motion play. He was the first coach to use blocking sleds and tackling dummies.

One of Stagg's coaching posts was at Springfield College in Massachusetts. A student on Amos Alonzo Stagg's gridiron squad was James Naismith, the person who invented the game of basketball.

Although Amos Alonzo Stagg is best remembered as a football coach who won 314 games, he was also instrumental in popularizing the sport of basketball throughout the Midwest. He is a member of both the Basketball Hall of Fame and the College Football Hall of Fame.

When it comes to football, you just can't sling any mud at the Garden State. On their way to victory in the 2008 Super Bowl, the New York Giants (who play their home games in East Rutherford, New Jersey) had to top the Green Bay Packers. The National Football Conference Championship game was played in Green Bay, Wisconsin. The Packers claimed the contest was a home game, but it was really the Giants who had the home-field advantage. The sod on Green Bay's Lambeau Field was grown at Tuckehoe Turf Farms in New Jersey. Tuckehoe Turf Farms in the Garden State provides sod for the Packers, the Cleveland Browns, and for the Boston Red Sox's home field, Fenway Park.

New Jersey also cuts an impressive figure in the "sweet science" of pugilism. Boxing's first million-gate was a bout between American heavyweight Jack Dempsey and French fighter Georges Carpentier. The fight was held in Jersey City, New Jersey, on July 2, 1921. Dempsey knocked out Carpentier in round four.

Another source of pride for New Jersey residents is the state's link to the sport of cycling. The U.S. Bicycling Hall of Fame is located in the Garden State.

New Jersey has produced or been home to a multitude of world champions, Olympic champions, and athletic icons from all phases of sport, from wrestling and weight lifting to swimming and skating. So when it comes to talking athletics, don't kid around with New Jersey. Garden State residents take their sports very seriously, even if they still don't know . . . "who's on first?"

RICHARD FRANCIS DENNIS BARRY

Basketball
Elizabeth, New Jersey
Born: March 28, 1944

Rick Barry was born in Elizabeth, New Jersey, and attended Roselle Catholic High School in Roselle Park, New Jersey. In high school, Barry was twice named to the New Jersey All-State basketball squad. He graduated in 1961 and enrolled at the University of Miami in Florida. The Miami Hurricanes were coached by Bruce Hale. Hale welcomed Barry to the Hurricanes family in more ways than one. Rick Barry starred on the basketball court for Coach Hale. Rick was also introduced to Bruce Hale's daughter, Pam, whom he later married.

In 1965, Rick Barry of the University of Miami led the nation in scoring. The slender six-foot-seven-inch-tall forward tallied 973 points in twenty-six games for an average of 37.4 points per hoop contest. Barry scored a total of 2,293 points over the span of his three-year college career. He averaged an impressive 29.8 points per game. Miami's Rick Barry was named a consensus All-American in 1965.

Barry bounced into the NBA in 1966 and blossomed into a pro scoring machine for the San Francisco Warriors. As a rookie, Rick filled up the hoop hole and averaged 25.7 points per pro contest. His sharp shooting secured him Rookie of the Year honors in the National Basketball Association.

In only his second season as a pro, Rick Barry skyrocketed to the top of the scoring chart in the NBA. In 1967, Barry shot bombs that exploded for 2,775 points in seventy-eight games for a league-topping 35.6 points per contest. He won the NBA scoring crown and played in the All-Star game, earning Most Valuable Player honors. In addition, Rick Barry, along with Warriors teammate Nate Thurmond, led San Francisco into the finals of the NBA Play-offs. However, the Philadelphia 76ers burst the Warriors' bubble, despite a fifty-five-point contribution by Rick Barry in game three of the championship series. Philadelphia, led by Wilt "the Stilt" Chamberlain, beat San Francisco four games to two to win the 1967 NBA title. Warriors' star Rick Barry averaged 40.8 points per game in that championship series

An interesting chain of events changed the course of Rick Barry's professional basketball career in 1967–68. The American Basketball Association (ABA), a rival of the NBA, had a team in Oakland, California. Former University of Miami coach Bruce Hale, who was Rick Barry's father-in-law, was hired as the head coach of the Oakland Oaks. The Oaks offered Barry a $75,000 contract to play in the ABA. That was a great deal of money at the time. The cash, plus the opportunity to play for his father-in-law, enticed Barry away from the San Francisco Warriors. Barry bolted from the NBA and set his shooting sites on an ABA scoring title. Unfortunately for Rick, Barry had one year remaining on his contract with the Warriors and was forced to sit out an entire season before playing for the Oaks.

Barry joined the Oakland Oaks as an active member of the squad for the1968–69 season. Rick promptly led the American Basketball Association in scoring by posting a 34.0 points per game average. Barry's leap of faith to the ABA was not without consequences. His father-in-law, Bruce Hale, moved from the court to the front office while Rick sat out his option year. Barry never played for his old college coach. Instead, he played for Alex Hannum, who took over on the floor for the Oakland Oaks. Barry also suffered a knee injury that limited the number of games he was able to play. Nevertheless, Rick Barry became the first player in basketball history to lead the NCAA, the NBA, and the ABA in scoring.

The Oakland Oaks were sold, and the team moved to Washington, DC, for the 1969–70 season. The Oaks were renamed the Washington Caps. The very next season, the team moved to Norfolk, Virginia, and became the Virginia Squires.

Rick Barry reluctantly played for the Caps and led Washington in the ABA Play-off by scoring 27.7 points per game. When the Caps relocated to Norfolk, Rick refused to repack his bags. Barry was traded to the New York Nets. Rick Barry returned to a familiar area. He'd grown up in the long shadows cast across the river into New Jersey by New York's skyscrapers. Barry played two seasons with the Nets. He fulfilled his ABA contract requirements and eventually returned to the NBA Warriors, who moved and were known as Golden State. In his four years in the ABA, Rick Barry tallied a total of 6,884 points.

In 1972, Rick Barry rejoined the West Coast Warriors. Nagging knee problems sapped some of Barry's scoring juice, and he labored through the next two seasons. In 1974–75, both Rick Barry and the Golden State Warriors were revitalized. Barry helped lead the Warriors to play-off victories over the Seattle SuperSonics and the Chicago Bulls. In the NBA Championship Series, the Warriors stunned the basketball world by sweeping the heavily favored Washington Bullets in four games. Rick Barry was named the Most Valuable Player of the championship series.

Rick Barry finished out his NBA career as a member of the Houston Rockets. He retired in 1980. Rick Barry played ten seasons in the NBA. He scored 18,395 points in 794 games for a 23.2 points per game average. Barry's combined NBA and ABA stats rank with the best who ever played the game of pro basketball. Rick scored 25,279 points in 1,020 regular-season games for a 27.8 per game average. He added 5,168 rebounds, 4,017 assists, and 1,104 steals. Although he was known for his scoring ability, Rick Barry was also a pinpoint passer and an outstanding defender. In 1974–75 he led the NBA with 228 steals.

Rick Barry was an eight-time NBA All Star (1966,1967,1973–78) and a four-time ABA All-Star (1969–1972). Barry is a member of the Basketball Hall of Fame and was named to the National Basketball Association's Fiftieth Anniversary All-Time Team.

BRUCE ROBERT BAUMGARTNER
Wrestling
Haledon, New Jersey
Born: November 2, 1960

New Jersey-bred Bruce Baumgartner is probably the best freestyle wrestler the Garden State has ever produced. Baumgartner's name is synonymous with success on the wrestling mat. New Jersey's premiere mat maestro won thirteen world championship and Olympic medals over the course of his amazing athletic career. He was also named the winner of the prestigious James E. Sullivan Award in 1995. The Sullivan Award is presented to an athlete "who by his or her performance, example and influence as an amateur has done the most during the year to advance the cause of sportsmanship". Bruce Baumgartner joined an elite clan of New Jersey athletes who have captured the Sullivan Award. They include Dick Button (ice skating), Debbie Meyer (swimming), Carl Lewis (track), Mary Decker (track), and Bill Bradley (basketball).

Strangely enough, Haledon's Bruce Baumgartner never won a New Jersey state wrestling championship in his days as a student at Manchester Regional High School. Bruce's best outing at the New Jersey State High School Wrestling Tournament was a third-place finish in the heavyweight division in 1978.

It was after high school that Bruce Baumgartner began his long and illustrious dominance as America's top heavyweight and later superheavyweight wrestler. Baumgartner enrolled at Indiana State University (ISU). Bruce placed second at the NCAA Championships his sophomore and junior years at ISU. As a senior, heavyweight Bruce Baumgartner steamrolled to an NCAA crown by going undefeated. Bruce won forty-four straight matches to pin down a National Collegiate Athletic Association Championship. Over the span of his college career, the heavyweight Hercules posted a spectacular record of 134 wins and 12 losses. Of Bruce's 134 victories, 73 were on falls, meaning that he pinned his opponent.

Baumgartner began his reign as the U.S. National Freestyle Heavyweight Champion in 1983. Bruce won the crown in 1983 and 1984.

Bruce made the U.S. Olympic squad and wrestled at the 1984 games, which were held in Los Angeles, California. Baumgartner was not seriously challenged by an opponent in any of his three matches. He completely dominated the superheavyweight division. Bruce beat Canada's Bob Molle 10–2 in the final to clinch the gold medal for himself and the United States.

In 1985, Bruce Baumgartner comfortably moved into the 186 pound weight class and went back to ruling the U.S. National Championship. He won the title twelve straight years from 1985 to 1996.

The powerful Garden State grappler also excelled in Olympic competition over that span of time. In 1988, at the Olympic Games in Seoul, South Korea, Baumgartner came home with a silver medal. In a strange twist of wrestling fate, Baumgartner was bested by David Gobezhishvilli of the Soviet Union in the finals. The U.S. champion had beaten the Soviet wrestler in all three of the previous meetings leading up to the Olympics. In their match at Seoul, Gobezhishvilli scored his first point only seventeen seconds into the match. The Soviet grappler gained another two points in the second period. Baumgartner tallied his lone point with ten seconds left in the final period. The match ended with Gobezhishvilli eking out a slim 3–1 victory over Baumgartner.

America's super superheavyweight rebounded at the 1992 Olympic Games at Barcelona, Spain. Bruce Baumgartner once again wrestled the gold from the grasps of the world's biggest and best grapplers. It was his second Olympic championship. At the 1996 Olympic Games in Atlanta, Georgia, Baumgartner won his fourth Olympic medal. This time Bruce's prize was a bronze medal for a third-place finish.

Most New Jersey wrestling experts agree that Bruce Baumgartner is at the top of the heap when it comes to rating the Garden State's best wrestlers. He also rates as one of the greatest wrestlers in U.S. history, and one of the best to ever grapple on the globe. In addition to the many awards and titles already mentioned, Baumgartner also won four Pan American Games medals and seven World Cup titles.

After retiring from mat competition, Bruce Baumgartner served as the Director of Athletics for Edinboro University of Pennsylvania.

Bruce Baumgartner–Courtesy Bruce Baumgartner

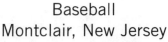

LAWRENCE P. "YOGI" BERRA
Baseball
Montclair, New Jersey
Born: May 12,1925

Yogi is the marvelous master of mind-boggling malaprops. The wacky way his tongue twists words and fractures phrases has tickled the funny bones of sports buffs for generations. He is the undisputed guru of goofy grammar. Only his astounding athletic accomplishments at the plate and behind it eclipse the brilliance of his great, but garbled use of English grammar.

Timely remarks from this sports sage include, "This is the earliest I've ever been late," and, "It gets late early out here."

Lawrence Peter Berra was born in Saint Louis, Missouri. He was raised in an Italian neighborhood known to locals as "the Hill." As a child, Larry Berra was called "Lawdie." However, his childhood buddies, who included future major-league catcher and TV baseball analyst Joe Garagiola, came up with a different nickname for their pal. They dubbed him "Yogi" because they thought young Berra resembled a Hindu holy man they'd seen in a movie.

Young Yogi Berra had his heart set on playing major-league baseball, even though his parents opposed their son's career goal. Berra's father was a bricklayer, and Pietro and Paulina Berra wanted their son to direct his energy into finding a normal job.

Nevertheless, Yogi Berra chased his dream and played baseball in various American Legion leagues. Yogi and his close friend Joe Garagiola often competed for the position of catcher. It wasn't long before pro scouts recognized that both young backstops had big-league potential. However, it was Joe Garagiola who was the first to ink a professional contract. In 1942, the Saint Louis Cardinals checked out Garagiola and Berra and decided Joe was a better risk. They passed on Yogi and signed Garagiola to a contract for five hundred dollars.

"You can observe a lot by watching," Yogi Berra once said. Yogi watched his childhood friend head for baseball's pro ranks, but was not discouraged by being overlooked by pro scouts because of his ability.

In 1943, at the age of seventeen, Yogi Berra was signed by the New York Yankees to play minor-league baseball. Berra received a five hundred dollar bonus and was paid ninety dollars a month to play professional baseball for a Yankees farm club. In the minor leagues, Yogi excelled at hitting, but needed work on his defensive skills as a catcher. Berra's behind-the-plate education was interrupted by World War II, and Yogi enlisted in the Navy. Berra was a gunners' mate and took part in the historic D-Day Invasion. After the war ended, Lawrence "Yogi" Berra returned to doing what he did best—playing baseball!

Yogi spent most of 1946 playing minor-league baseball and saw plenty of action behind the plate for the Newark Bears in New Jersey. At the end of the year, Yogi was summoned to serve time with the parent club in New York City. Twenty-one-year-old Yogi Berra played in seven games and collected eight hits in twenty-two at bats for a .364 batting average. Counted among those eight hits were two home runs and a double. Yogi also had four runs batted in. Yogi impressed Yanks manager, Joe McCarthy, by clubbing a home run in his first major-league game. Berra also picked up some key defensive tips from incumbent catcher Bill Dickey.

The year 1947 was one steeped in historic baseball significance. Outfielder Larry Doby joined the Cleveland Indians and became the first African American player in the American Leagues. The Boston Red Sox installed lights in Fenway Park. The New York Yankees and the Brooklyn Dodgers faced off in the World Series. Last, but not least, catcher Yogi Berra entered the major leagues full-time as a rookie catcher. Yogi played in 83 eighty-three games as a rookie and banged out 82 eighty-two hits in 293 at bats for a .280 batting average. He also bashed 11 eleven home runs and collected 54 fifty-four runs batted in.

In the third game of the World Series, which the Yankees lost to the Dodgers (9--8), Yogi Berra belted the first pinch -hit home run in World Series history. The Yankees, led by their stars Joe DiMaggio, Phil Rizzuto, and Ralph Houk, captured the World Series Ccrown for mManager Bucky Harris in six games.

Yogi was used as a catcher part- time during the 1947 and 1948 seasons. He often played in right field. Veteran Ralph Houk and Gus Niarhos also saw duty behind the plate. In 1949, Yankee Mmanager Casey Stengael appointed Yogi as the Yank's' steady starting catcher and hired former New York backstop Bill Dickey to tutor Berra in the fine points of calling a game and playing defense. Under the mentorship of Bill Dickey, Yogi Berra blossomed into a bona fide Bbig -lLeague backstop star. He once went 148 consecutive games without committing an error. He was also a whiz at throwing out base runners and calling shrewd pitches. Yogi was behind the plate for pitcher Don Larson's consummate "perfect game" against the Brooklyn Dodgers in the 1953 World Series.

However, it is Yogi Berra's incredible use of lumber in the batter's box which that elevated him to the stately status of a baseball immortal. Berra was a brute with a bat. He could hack with the best players to ever swing a stick. In 1948, he hit .305 by smashing 143 hits in 469 at bats. Yogi clubbed a total of 14 fourteen home runs, 10 ten triples, and 24 twenty-four doubles. He added 98 ninety-eight RBI's to his tally sheet that season.

His batting average dipped to .277 in 1949, but he blasted 20 twenty homers and drove in ninety-one91 runs. The next year he raised all of his numbers to eye-catching levels. In 1950, Yogi batted .322 and hit 28 twenty-eight fence- clearing round trippers. He also cracked the 100- mark level in RBI's by collecting 124 runs batted in. His total of 192 hits was second on the team only to shortstop Phil Rizzuto's 200 hits.

Yogi followed up his superlative diamond season in 1950 with an effort which that won him the American League's Most Valuable Player Award in 1951. Berra batted .294, clouted 27 twenty-seven home runs, and drove in 88 eighty-eight runs to earn the prestigious honor.

The year 1951 was an interesting footnote in Yankee history. In addition to Yogi's brilliant performance as a slugging backstop, it was the final season for Joe DiMaggio, baseball's famous Yankee Clipper. Joltin' Joe would no longer sail through center field in the Bronx dressed in Yankee pinstripes. His heir apparent was nineteen-year-old rookie sensation Mickey Mantle, who made his debut in pinstripes in 1951.

Yogi Berra repeated as the American League's Most Valuable Player in 1954. Berra hit .307 that season. He added 125 runs batted in and 22 home runs to his season output.

In 1955, Yogi was once again the league's top performer. He was named the Most Valuable Player in 1955, when he posted a .272 batting average, crashed 27 home runs, and drove in 108 runs.

Yogi continued to unleash the lumber against opposing pitchers. He was famous for swinging at any pitches he liked, even if they were out of the strike zone. He was known as a "bad ball" hitter, but a pitch can't be bad if the end result is a hit. Besides, Berra was a clutch hitter, who seldom struck out. A good example is his 1950 batting stats. Yogi was up 597 times and only struck out 12 times. In 1955, he was up 541 times and whiffed just 20 times. Berra came to the plate 482 times in 1957 and only K'ed 24 times. Yogi had an uncanny knack for putting the wood on the horsehide and making it fly. In 1956, Berra sent thirty pitches sailing into the stands. It was the second time he'd clouted thirty fence clearers in a year. (The first time was in 1952.)

Hitting-machine Yogi Berra continued to post solid seasons at the plate throughout his major-league career. In 2,120 games, Yogi had 2,148 hits and a career .285 batting average. He clubbed 358 home runs and amassed 1,430 runs batted in. In addition, Berra had 49 triples, 321 doubles, and scored 1,175 runs.

While Yogi Berra was plastering opposing pitching, the New York Yankees as a team won ten World Series crowns. Berra appeared in fourteen World Series competitions. He played in seventy-five World Series games. Yogi had seventy-one hits in 259 World Series at bats for a .274 batting average. His seventy-one hits are tops in World Series competition. Berra also bombed fifteen home runs over his career, which is second only to teammate Mickey Mantle's eighteen home runs. Yogi's World Series RBI total of thirty-nine is also only second to Mickey Mantle's total of forty runs batted in.

Yogi Berra's brilliant playing career ended after the 1963 season. Yogi's days as a hitter and catcher were history, but his baseball journey was not yet over. There were still diamond gems to be added to Yogi's sports treasure trove.

Yogi Berra was hired to manage the New York Yankees. He replaced Ralph Houk, who was named the Yankees' general manager. Yogi skippered the Yankees to the AL pennant and a berth in the World Series against the NL Championship Saint Louis Cardinals. The Cardinals, led by pitcher Bob Gibson and catcher Tim McCarver, beat the Yankees in a close, hard-fought, seven-game series.

Yogi was released and joined his former manager Casey Stengel with the New York Mets. Stengel was the Mets' skipper, and Yogi became a player-coach. Berra had nine at bats as a New York Met in 1965 and collected two hits, both singles.

In 1972, Yogi was named the manager of the New York Mets. He guided the team to the National League pennant in 1973 to become the third manager in major-league history to capture pennants in both leagues. He remained the Mets' manager for two more seasons.

Yogi Berra rejoined his beloved Yankees as a coach in 1976. He once again resumed the role of Yankee skipper in 1984. He remained with the Yankees through the early part of the 1985 season. His abrupt dismissal as the Yankees' manager by team owner George Steinbrenner caused hard feelings between the two pinstripe icons, which were not ironed out until some fifteen years later. Yogi Berra now has a plaque of honor in Yankee Stadium alongside other New York immortals.

Yogi Berra has resided in Montclair, New Jersey, for many, many years. His son, Dale Berra, played professional baseball for the Pittsburgh Pirates, the Houston Astros, and the New York Yankees. The Yogi Berra Museum and Learning Center and Yogi Berra Stadium (on the campus of Montclair State University) are located in the Garden State. Lawrence Peter "Yogi" Berra was elected to the Baseball Hall of Fame in 1972.

Yogi Berra serves as an inspiration for young baseball players. But in Yogi's own words, "If you can't copy him, don't imitate him."

Yogi Berra–Courtesy Yogi Berra/Yogi Berra Museum & Learning Center

MICHAEL BIBBY
Basketball
Cherry Hill, New Jersey
Born: May 13, 1978

There's an old adage that relates to heredity. The old adage, "Like father, like son," certainly ring true when it comes to the Bibby family. Offensively, NBA point guard Mike Bibby can do it all on a basketball floor. He's a remarkable ball handler who is a deadly shooter and a pinpoint passer. He's extremely athletic and amazing durable. Bibby is at his best when under pressure and the chips are down. He's also a bona fide chip off the old basketball block. Michael Bibby is the son of Henry Bibby. Mike's dad is a former UCLA and NBA star. Henry Bibby also coached basketball at the University of Southern California and in the National Basketball Association. When anyone talks b-ball around Mike and Henry, the *B* usually stands for Bibby.

Michael Bibby was born in Cherry Hill, New Jersey, but played high school basketball at Shadow Mountain High School in Phoenix, Arizona. Bibby was named the Arizona High School Player of the Year three successive times (1994, 1995, and 1996). The flashy point guard was named to the USA Today All-USA Team in 1996. He was selected to participate in the McDonalds All-America Game that same season.

After a phenomenal high school career, Mike Bibby chose to stay home to play for Coach Lute Olsen at the University of Arizona. The six foot one inch, 190-pound point guard starred for the Wildcats as a freshman. Bibby was named the Pac-10 Conference's Freshman of the Year in 1996–97. Mike also helped the Arizona Wildcats capture a National Championship in 1996–97. In the NCAA Basketball Championship Game, Arizona topped Kentucky 84–79 in overtime to win the national college hoops crown. Mike Bibby tallied twenty points in the title contest.

Mike Bibby followed up his fantastic freshman year with a super sophomore season. He was selected as a First Team Pac-10 Player of the Year in 1997–98. Mike Bibby started all sixty-nine games of his two-year college career at the University of Arizona.

Bibby decided to go pro after his second season of college basketball. He was selected by the Vancouver Grizzlies in the first round and was the second player picked in the 1998 NBA draft.

The Grizzlies' young rookie guard posted favorable stats in an NBA season shortened by a labor dispute. Bibby averaged 13.2 points and 6.5 assists per game in his first year as a pro. He was rewarded for his efforts by being named to the NBA All-Rookie First Team in 1998–99. Bibby led the Grizzlies in assists (665) and steals (132) in 2000–01. The following season, the Grizzlies moved to Memphis, and Mike Bibby was traded to the Sacramento Kings. In 2001–02 the reliable point guard helped guide the Kings into the Western Conference finals, which they dropped to the Los Angeles Lakers.

Bibby had a solid season in 2002–03, despite being hampered by a series of injuries. He played in only fifty-five games, but averaged 15.9 points per game.

In 2003–04, Mike Bibby had a hot hand against the Dallas Mavericks in the first round of the NBA Play-offs. Mike scored a career play-off best total of thirty-six points in the contest.

The 2004–05 NBA season turned into a family affair for the veteran Kings' point guard. Mike Bibby was joined in the Sacramento backcourt by his cousin, Eddie House.

Bibby's career stats continued to pile up over the next two NBA seasons. In 2006–07, Mike became the sixty-first pro star in NBA history to reach the lofty totals of ten thousand career points and four thousand career assists.

The Atlanta Hawks acquired Mike Bibby from the Sacramento Kings in mid-February of 2008. The Hawks planned to pair the steady and reliable Mike Bibby with their all-star shooting guard, Joe Johnson.

"It'll be like a one-two punch in the backcourt," Hawks' coach Mike Woodson told the press after the trade was announced. Bibby proved to be an instant welcome addition to the Hawks' roster. In his first two home games for Atlanta, Mike Bibby recorded two double doubles. In a crucial game against the New York Knicks on February 29, 2008, Bibby had eleven points and ten assists in helping the Hawks record a 99–93 victory over the Knicks.

In 2007–08, the Atlanta Hawks made the NBA Play-offs for the first time since 1999. Down the final stretch of the season, the Hawks won thirteen of twenty games to lock up the final play-off spot in the Eastern Conference. Point guard Mike Bibby, along with Joe Johnson and Mike Woodson were a big part of that success.

Mike Bibby's incredible steady offensive output no matter where he plays is no surprise. Bibby, who has averaged over sixteen points per game over the course of his NBA career, has great blood. After all, his dad was a terrific basketball player, and it's one more case of "like father, like son" in the wide world of sports.

 Mike Bibby–Courtesy Rocky Widner/NBAE/Getty Images

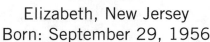

CAROL BLAZEJOWSKI
Basketball
Elizabeth, New Jersey
Born: September 29, 1956

Carol Blazejowski was one of women's basketball's first stars, along with Nancy Lieberman, Ann Meyer, and Anne Donovan. Carol was nicknamed "the Blaze," and she heated things up on the basketball court by firing her sizzling jump shot with amazing accuracy.

In the early 1970s, women's basketball was searching for its niche in the national sports spotlight. Young Carol Blazejowski was court-schooled on New Jersey playgrounds in hotly contested hoop contests against mostly male foes. She taught herself how to shoot a jump shot by watching pro players on television. Carol developed her own unique and natural style of play, which she perfected in pickup games against guys.

It wasn't until her senior year at Cranford High School in Cranford, New Jersey, that she finally went out for her school team. It was Carol's introduction to organized women's basketball, and as the old saying states, a star was born!

After graduating from high school, the five foot ten inch forward enrolled at Montclair State College in New Jersey. Carol quickly became the college game's newest scoring sensation. The Blaze was selected for the Women's Basketball All-America Team in 1976, 1977, and 1978.

Blazejowski led the nation in scoring in 1976–77 by averaging an amazing 33.5 points per game. She also led Montclair State to a number-eight ranking in the AP Women's Basketball National Final Poll.

In 1977, Carol was a key player on the U.S. Women's Team, which played in the World University Games. Blazejowski was the top scorer for the U.S. team and tallied 38 points in a tough loss to the powerful Soviet Union squad.

During the 1977–78 college season, the Blaze regularly burned the opposition with her hot shooting to once again top the nation in scoring with a scorching 38.6 points per game average. In a game against Queens College at Madison Square Garden in 1978, Carol Blazejowski poured in a stunning total of fifty-two points. In fact, the Blaze scored forty or more points in each of her last three games, to lead Montclair to a number-four ranking in the final AP Women's Basketball Polls in 1978.

In all, Carol "the Blaze" Blazejowski collected 3,199 total points in her college career, and that was in the days before the three-point shot. Carol was aptly rewarded for her outstanding efforts as a collegian by being named the winner of the inaugural Wade Trophy, which is presented annually to the nation's finest collegiate woman player.

After her college career concluded, Carol Blazejowski decided to retain her amateur status in the hope of playing on the 1980 Olympic Basketball Team. Women's pro basketball was still developing fan support and national media exposure at that time.

Carol played two seasons of AAU basketball with the Allentown (Pennsylvania) Crestettes. In 1979, the Blaze was the top scorer on the U.S. National Team that won the World Championship.

In 1980, Blazejowski was named to the U.S. Olympic Team, but her dreams of capturing a gold medal at the games disappeared when the United States government decided to boycott the 1980 Summer Olympics in Moscow (U.S.S.R.).

Carol "the Blaze" Blazejowski finally turned pro and signed a contract with the New Jersey Gems of the Women's Basketball League (WBL). Blazejowski signed a three-year deal for $150,000 to become the highest-paid player in the league. However, the Women's Basketball League went out of business a year later. In 1984, Blazejowski made a second attempt at a pro career with the reorganized Women's American Basketball Association. However, once again the league failed to survive.

Carol Blazejowski then retired as a player and worked for the National Basketball Association. In 1994, Carol "the Blaze" Blazejowski was enshrined in the Basketball Hall of Fame. Blazejowski was named the vice president and general manager of the WNBA's New York Liberty team in 1997. Two years later, in 1999, Carol Blazejowski was inducted into the inaugural class of the Women's Basketball Hall of Fame.

Carol Blazejowski–
Courtesy Montclair State
University Sports
Information

*Montclair State
University's
Outstanding
Female Athlete
Aware is named in
honor of Carol
Blazejowski*

Carol Blazejowski–Courtesy Montclair State University Sports Information

GARY BRACKETT
Football
Glassboro, New Jersey
Born: May 23, 1980

In football, there is an old saying among players and coaches. A gridiron wise man once said, "Never judge a football player by his size. Judge a football player by the size of his heart."

Glassboro's Gary Brackett has the heart of a lion when it comes to the sport of football. Brackett, who is five feet eleven inches tall and weighs in at about 235 pounds, is not the usual mammoth linebacker who prowls the middle NFL turf between defensive linemen and defensive backs. However, do not dare to think Gary Brackett isn't big enough to play big-time football. Gridiron experts tried that once before, and Gary Brackett made them eat their words.

Brackett was a star athlete at Glassboro High School in New Jersey. College scouts said he was quick enough, smart enough, strong enough, and tough enough to play Division 1-A college football. The only thing that kept them from offering him a full scholarship was his size. Brackett wasn't big enough by modern standards.

The harsh rejection of Gary's potential as a big-time football athlete based solely on a yardstick principle provided immense motivation for Gary Brackett. He enrolled at Rutgers University and tried out for the team as a walk-on. Eventually, Brackett clawed his way into the starting lineup as a middle linebacker. He earned the admiration of the Rutgers coaches and the respect of his fellow Scarlet Knight players.

In 2001, junior Gary Brackett was named a Rutgers football captain. The following season, Brackett was voted defensive captain for a second straight year. Senior Gary Brackett responded by excelling at his middle linebacker position in 2002. Brackett led the team with 130 tackles, including 82 unassisted tackles. He was named the Scarlet Knights' Most Valuable Player and was a First Team All-East choice.

After graduation, middle linebacker Gary Brackett was overlooked by pro scouts because of his size. He was not selected in the National Football League draft, but was signed to a free-agent contract by the Indianapolis Colts.

Brackett had to overcome the odds against an undersized player making the final roster of an NFL team. It was the same battle he'd fought and won in college. Once again, Gary Brackett was the victor. He earned a spot on the Colts' squad. For two seasons, Brackett labored tirelessly on special teams. He also saw spot duty as a backup linebacker. Finally, in 2005, Brackett's patience, perseverance, and overall ability paid dividends.

Gary Brackett became the Indianapolis Colts' starting middle linebacker in 2005. His first full season as a starter on defense was a triumphant gridiron debut. Brackett quickly showcased his athletic talent and his instincts for the ball. He made a total of 131 tackles and had three pass interceptions.

In 2006, Gary Brackett had 123 tackles and helped the Colts coast to an AFC Championship.

In Super Bowl XLI (played February 4, 2007), the Indianapolis Colts took on the NFC Champion Chicago Bears. The Colts, led by their star quarterback, Peyton Manning, topped the Bears by a score of 29–17. Indianapolis' head coach, Tony Dungy, became the first black NFL coach to record a Super Bowl win. No one on the Colts savored the victory more than middle linebacker Gary Brackett.

In 2007, Gary Brackett received another big honor. He was named the captain of the Colts' defense. Although his size remains the same, football player Gary Brackett's accomplishments continue to grow in stature.

Gary Brackett–
Courtesy Indianapolis
Colts Football

In 2002 Gary Brackett made 130 tackles as the Defensive Captain of the Rutgers football team

Gary Brackett–Courtesy Indianapolis Colts Football

JAMES J. BRADDOCK
Boxing
West New York/North Bergen, New Jersey
Born: June 7, 1905

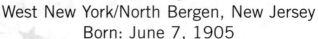

It's been said that he was one of boxing's most decent and honorable men. He was a no nonsense guy in life, and that's the way he faced opponents in the ring. Jim Braddock was a stand-up straight fighter with a punishing right jab and a deadly right-hand punch. They dubbed him "the Bergen Bulldog" and "the Pride of New Jersey." He is best known by the same name of the famous fight movie that immortalized his life. Heavyweight boxing champion James J. Braddock will be forever recalled as "the Cinderella Man".

James Walter Braddock was born on the West Side of New York City, in the area known as "Hell's Kitchen." When James was only nine months old, his father moved the Braddock family across the Hudson River to West New York, New Jersey. Jimmy Braddock grew up in a poor Irish family that valued honesty, truth, and fair play. As a youth, Braddock dreamed about playing football at the University of Notre Dame, but he soon channeled all of his athletic abilities into a sport known to insiders as the sweet science—boxing!

Jim Braddock dropped out of school at age sixteen. At the time, he stood six feet tall and weighed 175 pounds. Braddock adopted the name James J. Braddock to use in the ring. He admired boxing champions James J. Corbett and James J. Jeffries and thought adding a *J* to his name might bring him some luck in the ring. Luck did seem to smile on the young pugilist, who was sometimes called "the Pride of the Irish" in addition to a slew of other nicknames.

James J. Braddock began his boxing career as an amateur with impressive results. He won the amateur light heavyweight crown of New Jersey. He then stood six feet two inches tall and weighed 195 pounds. Braddock moved up to the heavyweight division and captured another championship. Finally, at age twenty-one, James J. Braddock turned professional.

Braddock's style was straightforward. He could take a hard punch and could deliver a solid knockout blow. He wasn't a muss-'em-up, slug-it-out brawler, nor was he a fancy-footwork, stick-and-dance boxer. Braddock was just plain hard-nosed and leather tough in the ring. When he fought, he stood tall and fought hard until the final bell. James J. Braddock was a gutsy guy who never paid any attention to the odds against him.

Jim Braddock also had good fight guidance. His manager was Max Gould, a shrewd and experienced man when it came to the business side of boxing. Braddock and Gould had first met when Jim was working out at Jeannette's Gym in Hoboken, New Jersey.

In Braddock's first year as a pro, he won sixteen straight fights. Eleven of those victories were by knockouts. Some fight experts considered Braddock's sixteen wins to be hollow victories. Most of Braddock's early opponents were no-name boxers. When Jim Braddock plastered tough guy Pete Latzo in 1927, the critics quickly quieted down. Latzo had a fine ring reputation, and Braddock broke Pete's jaw en route to earning a victory.

Nevertheless, the odds were stacked against James J. Braddock in his big fight against highly regarded Tuffy Griffith later that same year. Braddock astonished fight experts by picking apart Griffith and winning the hard-fought bout.

Unfortunately, Braddock's rising boxing balloon was quickly deflated when he lost to seasoned fighter Leo Lomski a short time later. Braddock bounced back with a big win over former light heavyweight champion Jimmy Slattery. The victory was a huge upset, and once again, boxing's hierarchy paid heed to the progress of Jimmy Braddock, the quiet Irish boxer.

In 1929, manager Max Gould signed Braddock to meet skillful fighter Tommy Loughran in Yankee Stadium. It was a huge fight for big money. If Braddock won, a shot at the heavyweight championship held by Primo Carnera might be in order.

Braddock did not fight well. Loughran controlled the pace of the fight from start to finish. During the bout, Braddock fractured his hands and couldn't throw a hard punch. James J. Braddock lost the fight, and with it a chance at a championship match. He also lost his confidence.

Jimmy Braddock went into a nosedive. He lost to Leo Lomski in a return match. He lost to boxer John Henry Lewis. He lost to Slapsie Maxie Rosenbloom, a fighter who went on to have a Hollywood career as an actor.

Braddock sank into a deep depression, and so did America. In 1933, most Americans were out of a job and penniless. Counted among them was James J. Braddock, who could no longer earn a living as a prizefighter. He and his manager, Max Gould, had parted company. Jimmy Braddock was forced to earn a living any way he could in order to support his wife and three children. The Braddock family lived in a run-down neighborhood in North Bergen, New Jersey. Jimmy Braddock worked on the New Jersey docks, unloading and loading cargo. His days as a boxer seemed over. Braddock couldn't even earn enough money to feed his family. He had to beg, borrow, and collect government relief money.

In 1934, Lady Luck once again smiled on boxer James J. Braddock. Primo Carnera was set to defend his heavyweight crown against top contender Max Baer, a fierce fighter known for his eccentric antics in the ring. Some sportswriters dubbed the contender "Madcap Maxie Baier." Others labeled him "the Magnificent Screwball.".

Thanks to the Carnera-Baer bout, Jim Braddock got the rare opportunity to revive his comatose ring career. The fight's promoter needed a no-name boxer to face off against an up-and-coming contender named John "Corn" Griffin in a preliminary bout. The promoter needed someone who would put on a good show, but didn't stand much of a chance against Griffin. Braddock's old manager, Max Gould, heard about the opening on the card and begged the promoter to give Braddock the fight. Both Gould and Braddock were down-and-out thanks to the Depression. Reluctantly, the promoter agreed.

When Gould told Braddock about the deal, the news was like manna from heaven. Braddock's family was starving, and he desperately needed cash for bills, rent, and food.

Once again, James J. Braddock was a huge underdog. The odds were more than six to one against him. As in the past, the experts underestimated the willpower of the tenacious Bergen Bulldog, Jim Braddock. Braddock unleashed a barrage of blows that battered Corn Griffin into cornmeal. By the third round, Griffin was pulverized, and the referee stopped the bout, declaring Jimmy Braddock the winner. Braddock was back.

The only bigger fight news than Braddock's victory that night was Max Baer's merciless thumping carnage of Primo Carnera in the championship bout. Max Baer, the Magnificent Screwball, had been crowned the new king of heavyweights.

James Braddock was not a royal contender at the time, but he was no longer boxing's court jester. There was nothing humorous about Braddock's miraculous comeback. Braddock went on to beat boxer John Henry Lewis, which evened an old ring debt. He beat a very tough Art Lasky in fifteen bloody rounds. Before long, twenty-nine-year-old Jim Braddock was the number-two contender for the heavyweight crown. Famous writer Damon Runyon dubbed Braddock the Cinderella Man for obvious reasons. Everyone wondered if the Cinderella Man would get a shot at Max Baer and the heavyweight crown.

Germany's Max Schmeling was the number-one contender. It was suggested that Braddock and Schmeling fight to determine who would get a title shot. When Schmeling declined the offer, Jimmy Braddock got a title bout against heavyweight champion Max Baer.

The highly publicized meeting between the Cinderella Man and the Magnificent Screwball took place on June 13, 1935, in New York, before thirty-five thousand fans. Max Baer was a ten-to-one favorite over Braddock. Fans rooted for Braddock, but few actually believed he could win. Baer was younger, bigger, and had a longer reach by six inches. Most experts predicted Max Baer would dispose of Jim Braddock by round three. A few ring pundits actually believed Baer might fatally beat Braddock into a bloody pulp.

James J. Braddock proved the experts wrong again. He fought a masterful fight, carefully avoiding Baer's explosive right-hand punches. Round after round, Braddock peppered the champion with punches and then boxed his way out of trouble. In an amazing exhibition of smart boxing, Jim Braddock turned the tide against Max Baer. When the fight ended after fifteen rounds, Jim Braddock was alive and well. It was the king who'd suffered a fate worse than death. Max Baer had lost the heavyweight crown. Jim Braddock became the new heavyweight champion. Braddock's amazing victory was the greatest upset in the history of boxing.

James J. Braddock held the heavyweight title until 1937. On June 22, 1937, Braddock battled Joe Louis, "the Brown Bomber," for the crown. Jim Braddock was greatly overmatched by Louis, one of boxing's best fighters. This time, the odds really were against Braddock. Louis battered Braddock to the point where the Bergen Bulldog's manager wanted to halt the fight. The Bergen Bulldog refused to let Max Gould do so. "I want to go out like a champion," Braddock told his manager. "I want to be carried out."

Joe Louis knocked out Jim Braddock in the eighth round of their championship fight. The Cinderella Man ceased to be the Heavyweight Champion of the World. However, he never ceased to be respected as a fighter and as a person.

James Walter J. Braddock died November 29, 1974, at the age of sixty-nine. He went out as a champion. Braddock was named to the International Boxing Hall of Fame in 2001. He joined his old ring adversaries Max Baer and Joe Louis, who were named to the Boxing Hall of Fame in 1995 and 1990 respectively.

WILLIAM WARREN "BILL" BRADLEY
Basketball
Verona, New Jersey
Born: July 28, 1943

He was known as "Dollar Bill," the player who almost always made the money shot when the game was on the line. He was also an Eagle Scout, a Rhodes scholar, a United States Senator from New Jersey, and a presidential candidate. Basketball star Bill Bradley epitomized the term *scholar athlete*.

William Bradley was born in Crystal City, Missouri. As a youngster, he worked tirelessly to improve his basketball skills. Bradley was blessed with exceptional peripheral vision, which enhanced his ability as an athlete. It was a combination of God-given athleticism, determination, and endless practice that produced amazing results on the basketball court for Bill Bradley. Bradley scored 3,068 points in high school and twice earned High School All-America honors. His court accomplishments made Bill Bradley a prime candidate for big-time college recruiters. Bradley fielded seventy-five scholarship offers. He passed up Duke University to attend Princeton University in New Jersey.

Bill Bradley played for legendary hoops mentor Butch van Breda Kolff at Princeton and blossomed into a bona fide all-American basketball star.

Bill set a record by making fifty-seven successive free throws as a freshman. As a super sophomore, Bradley averaged 27.3 points and 12.2 rebounds per game. In an NCAA tournament game against Saint Joseph's in Philadelphia, Bradley tallied forty points.

Junior Bill Bradley proved to be a Princeton Tiger no defender could tame on the b-ball court. He scored fifty-one points in a game against Harvard in 1964 and poured in forty-one points in a court contest against Michigan. Bill Bradley averaged 33.1 points per game in 1964 and earned himself a berth on the U.S. Olympic Basketball squad.

Bradley was named captain of the Olympic Team. The U.S. squad went on to win a gold medal at the 1964 Olympic Games.

Bill Bradley's senior season at Princeton proved to be the pinnacle of his college career. He was named an All-American for a third straight year. Princeton advanced to the Final Four of the NCAA Basketball Tournament with the help of their six foot five inch, 205-pound, sharpshooting forward. Princeton finished third. In the Tigers' NCAA contest against Wichita State in the consolation game, Bill Bradley filled up the hoop with fifty-eight points.

In 1965, Princeton's Bill Bradley was unanimously named the College Basketball Player of the Year. He also won the James E. Sullivan Award as the top amateur athlete in the United States. Bradley was the first college basketball star to win the Sullivan. He concluded his college career with a total of 2,503 points. Bill averaged 30.2 points per game in college.

Bill Bradley graduated with honors from Princeton University and was awarded a Rhodes scholarship to the University of Oxford in England. Bradley was also named the number-one pick of the New York Knicks in the 1965 NBA player draft. Bill Bradley chose to attend Oxford rather than sign with the Knickerbockers.

In 1967, Bill Bradley completed his studies at Oxford and returned home to play in the National Basketball Association. He signed with the Knicks, but found it difficult to rekindle the fire that blazed inside him as a college scorer. His hot hand as a shooter cooled; he tallied only 360 points as a pro rookie and averaged only 8 points a game.

Dollar Bill slowly regained his star status, but never averaged more than 16.1 points per game (1972–73) in the NBA. In 1966–70, he was part of a phenomenal Knicks team that won the NBA crown. It was New York's first championship in the National Basketball Association. The Knickerbockers won a second NBA title in 1972–73, thanks to the efforts of Knick stars Willis Reed, Walt Frazier, Dave De Busschere, Earl Monroe, Phil Jackson, Bill Bradley, and others. The 1972–73 NBA season was Bill Bradley's best year as a professional. He scored a total of 1,319 points (a 16.1 per game average) that season and pulled down 301 rebounds. He also had a career high of 367 assists. Bradley was named to the NBA All-Star Game that year.

Bill Bradley retired from pro basketball in 1977. He tallied a total of 9,217 points. He added 2,354 rebounds, 2,533 assists, and 209 steals to his ten-year career totals. Dollar Bill also had 1,222 points, 333 rebounds, 263 assists, and 9 steals in NBA Play-off competition. Bill Bradley was elected to the Basketball Hall of Fame in 1982. His jersey number, twenty-four, was retired by the New York Knicks in 1984.

In 1978, Bill Bradley decided to run for the U.S. Senate in New Jersey and was elected to office. Bradley served until 1996, when he opted not to run for reelection. Bill Bradley ran in the 2000 presidential primaries, but lost the nomination to Al Gore. Dollar Bill Bradley now resides in Verona, New Jersey, and is still active in politics and social causes.

Princeton University star Bill Bradley (center-seated) won a gold medal as a member of the 1964 U.S. Olympic basketball team

Bill Bradley–Courtesy USA Basketball

CHRIS CAMPBELL
Wrestling
Westfield, New Jersey
Born: unavailable

One would be tempted to label New Jersey's Chris Campbell the classic comeback kid of freestyle wrestling, except for the fact that Campbell made his remarkable reappearance in the world class wrestling competition at the age of thirty-four.

A superbly conditioned individual, Chris Campbell enjoyed a successful mat career as a youngster, a teenager, a young man, and later, as a middle-aged athlete.

Chris Campbell was a superstar grappler at Westfield High School during the early 1970s. Campbell was a fiercely competitive wrestler who combined speed and strength with flawless technical skills. After winning a New Jersey state wrestling title, Campbell enrolled at the collegiate monastery of mat masters, the University of Iowa, where he was mentored by fabled wrestling immortals Gary Kurdelmeier and Dan Gable.

The University of Iowa's legendary record in NCAA wrestling may never be eclipsed. Iowa was the NCAA Champion eleven times from 1975 to 1986. From 1975 up to and including the year 2000, the University of Iowa won the national team title a total of twenty times. The Hawkeyes' domination of college mat action is beyond doubt. New Jersey's Chris Campbell, who normally wrestled at 180.5 pounds, was part of the Iowa recipe for success. In 1976 and 1977, Chris contributed by winning national titles.

In 1980, Campbell made the U.S. Olympic team, but could not wrestle because of the United States' boycott of the Moscow Games. Campbell became a World Champion in 1981 and went on to become a four-time World Cup winner. When he captured the gold medal at the World Cup Competition in Skopje, Yugoslavia, in 1981, Chris Campbell was also named the tournament's most technical wrestler, an esteemed award.

Campbell was the U.S. National Champion in 1983. He attempted to earn a berth on the 1984 U.S. Olympic Team, but a string of injuries hampered his progress and prevented Campbell from realizing his lifelong dream of competing at an Olympiad.

Chris Campbell stepped off of the mat as a competitor and set his sights on other goals. He obtained a law degree. He worked as an assistant wrestling coach at Iowa, Iowa State, Cornell, and Syracuse. Campbell had a good life, but still yearned to test his strength and wrestling skills on a competitive level. The urge to wrestle still burned deep within him. There was no way to extinguish the fire and only one way to fuel the flames. Wrestle!

Chris Campbell shocked and rocked the wrestling world when he chose to make a competitive comeback in 1989 at thirty-four years of age. Campbell amazed the experts by climbing to a number-two ranking among U.S. wrestlers in 1989. Campbell's unbelievable comeback continued in 1990. He won a second United States National Championship that year and was named the outstanding wrestler of the tournament. At the World Championship in Tokyo, Japan, Campbell wrestled his way to a second-place finish and was awarded a silver medal.

Chris Campbell completed his astonishing comeback by making the 1992 Olympic squad when he was thirty-seven years old. Campbell competed in the Olympics at Barcelona, Spain, and battled his way to a bronze-medal victory. He was the oldest-known United States wrestler to ever win a medal in Olympic competition.

In addition to his NCAA titles and world and Olympic victories, Chris Campbell also earned numerous other freestyle wrestling titles. He finally retired from active competition after the 1992 Olympics.

Campbell is still active in the sport he loves. He works as a corporate attorney, but has served on the USA Wrestling Board of Directors and the U.S. Olympic Committee.

Chris Campbell–Courtesy University of Iowa Photo Services

MILTON GARY CAMPBELL
Track and Field
Plainfield, New Jersey
Born: December 9, 1933

The man who wins the Olympic decathlon is touted as the world's greatest athlete, and rightfully so. The decathlon consists of ten vastly different track-and-field events held over the course of a two-day period. On day one, the athletes compete in the 100-meter dash, the long jump, the shot put, the high jump, and the 400-meter run. The decathlon concludes on day two, after competitions in the 110-meter hurdles, the discus throw, the pole vault, the javelin, and the 1,500-meter run. Points are awarded in each event, and the athlete with the most total points is declared the champion. Past winners of the decathlon read like a who's who of the world's finest athletes. They include Jim Thorpe, Glenn Morris, and Bob Mathias.

New Jersey native, Milt Campbell, who was born in Plainfield, New Jersey, is counted among the world's best, thanks to a below-par performance in the Olympic event of his first choice.

Milt Campbell excelled in all sports in high school, but experienced his greatest successes as a swimmer, a fullback in football, and a hurdler on the track team. Campbell won All-State notices in football and earned numerous state championship titles in track and field. Young Milt rapidly developed into a world-class hurdler, and after his high school graduation, enrolled at Indiana University.

Milt Campbell was just eighteen years old when he attempted to earn a berth on the United States Olympic Team, which would compete in Helsinki in 1952. Milt's plan was to make the Olympic squad as a hurdler. However, Campbell didn't qualify. He finished fourth in the hurdle finals, which left him on the outside looking in.

"I was stunned," Campbell said afterward. "But then God seemed to reach into my heart and tell me he didn't want me to compete in the hurdles, but in the decathlon."

Milt Campbell made the 1952 Olympic Team as a decathlete. At the 1952 Olympic Games, Campbell clashed with the best of the best athletes from the far corners of the globe. The young sports star from Plainfield, New Jersey, racked up an impressive total of 6,975 points. His point accumulation was second only to gold-medal-defending decathlete Bob Mathias of the United States. Mathias amassed a total of 7,887 points to capture his second straight gold medal in Olympic decathlon competition. Milt Campbell finished in second place and took home the silver medal in 1952.

As Campbell waited four years for the next Olympiad, he played a little football at Indiana University and competed on the track team. In 1953, Milt won the AAU Decathlon Championship. In 1955, Campbell captured the NCAA and the AAU 120-Yard Hurdle championships.

When it was time for the 1956 Olympics in Melbourne, Australia, twenty-two-year-old Milt Campbell was more than ready to challenge for the title of world's best athlete. His toughest competition would come from the Soviet Union's Vassily Kuznyetsov and Uno Palu. Fellow American Rafer Johnson would also be a fierce competitor.

Milt Campbell quickly proved that he stood alone as the world's top athlete of the 1956 Olympic Games. He led from start to finish in the decathlon competition. He iced a victory after recording a splendid time of 14.0 in the 110-meter hurdles event. Nevertheless, Campbell never eased up. He ran 4:50.6 in the 1,500 meters to take first place in the decathlon's final event.

Milt Campbell totaled 7,937 points to take home the gold. Fellow American Rafer Johnson won the silver medal with a total of 7,587 points. Vassily Kuznyetsov of the Soviet Union earned the bronze medal with a total of 7,465 points.

Milt Campbell's triumph at the 1956 Olympic Games is recalled by many as an outstanding exhibition of pure athletic talent. Campbell could do it all when it came to sports, and his two Olympic medals in the decathlon prove that fact.

Milt Campbell later embarked on a pro-football career. He played briefly in the National Football League with the Cleveland Browns and in the Canadian Football League with the Montreal Alouettes. Along with Rafer Johnson, Bill Toomey, and Bruce Jenner, Milt Campbell is regarded as one of America's all-time finest athletes.

In 1989, Milt Campbell was named to the National Track and Field Hall of Fame. He was inducted into the U.S. Olympic Hall of Fame in 1992.

RICHARD ALDO CERONE
Baseball
Newark, New Jersey
Born: May 19, 1954

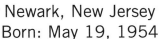

He was a guy blessed with a myriad of marvelous attributes. New Jersey-born baseball sensation Rick Cerone had Herculean physical qualities and the looks of Adonis. He was also extremely intelligent and possessed a shrewd business sense.

Cerone's rugged good looks and his keen mind sometimes overshadowed the fact that he spent eighteen seasons in the major leagues at a somewhat less than glamorous position.

The five foot eleven inch, 190-pound Seton Hall alum spent most of his major-league career doing dirty work behind the dish. Squatting behind home plate in the big leagues is no soft job, so you can add still another remarkable quality to Rick Cerone's many attributes. He was tough, too.

Rick Cerone was born in Newark, New Jersey, and after a stellar high school sports career, enrolled at New Jersey's Seton Hall University.

Seton Hall is an esteemed institution of higher education and has a national reputation for producing excellent sports teams, especially in basketball and baseball. Former Seton Hall Pirate baseball players who've gone on to star in the major leagues include Craig Biggio, Jack Morris, Mo Vaughn, and John Valentin.

Catcher Rick Cerone excelled on the diamond for Seton Hall in the early 1970s, winning all-star awards and attracting the attention of a multitude of major-league scouts.

In the 1975 amateur baseball draft, Cerone was selected by the Cleveland Indians in the first round. In fact, Rick Cerone was the seventh player picked overall. Cerone signed with "the Tribe" and at age twenty-one spent only a brief time in the minors. He was summoned up to the parent club on August 17, 1975, and appeared in seven games for the Indians. In 1976, Rick again appeared in seven major-league contests in Cleveland and was then dealt to the Toronto Blue Jays, who joined the American League in 1977.

Cerone provided the Jays with a steady glove behind the plate from 1977 to 1979. Rick appeared in a total of 255 games for Toronto.

The New York Yankees came calling in 1980. They were searching for the right kind of catcher to replace all-star backstop and team captain Thurman Munson, who had tragically perished in a plane crash the year before. Rick

Cerone donned Yankee pinstripes and joined a celebrated New York squad that included Reggie Jackson, Lou Piniella, Bobby Mercer, and Willie Randolph.

Rick Cerone had his best year in the big leagues during the 1980 season. Cerone collected 144 hits in 519 at bats for a solid .277 batting average. He blasted thirty doubles, four triples, and fourteen home runs. Rick added eighty-five RBIs and even had a stolen base. He also scored seventy runs.

In 1981, the New York Yankees, managed by Bob Lemon, captured the American League crown, but lost to skipper Tommy LaSorda's Los Angeles Dodgers in the World Series. Cerone contributed to the Yankees' American League success by hitting .244 in eighty-nine games.

Rick Cerone remained a member of the fabled Bronx Bombers until 1984, when he was traded to the Atlanta Braves for Brian Fisher. The Braves swapped Cerone to the Milwaukee Brewers in 1986.

The former Seton Hall star put up decent numbers at the plate and added stability behind it for the Brewers. He appeared in sixty-eight games and had a .259 batting average with fourteen doubles and four home runs.

Cerone rejoined the Yankees in 1987 as a free agent. He manned the dish for over one hundred games that season. In 1988, he deserted the Bronx for Boston and played for the Red Sox. Rick posted the third-best batting average of his major-league career when he hit .269 in Beantown. After a second season in Fenway Park, he once again returned to Yankee Stadium, the house that (Babe) Ruth built.

In 1990, Rick Cerone appeared in only forty-nine games, but posted a .302 batting average.

At the conclusion of the 1990 baseball season, Cerone once again moved to a new team. This time he hopped over to the National League and skipped across town to Shea Stadium as a member of the New York Mets. Cerone appeared behind the plate in ninety games in 1991 and posted a more-than-respectable .273 batting average in his only year as a Met.

Rick Cerone concluded his playing career as a member of the Montreal Expos in 1992. He saw limited action, appearing in only thirty-three games.

In his eighteen years as a big leaguer, New Jersey's Rick Cerone blasted 998 hits in 4,069 at bats for a career .245 batting average. He hit 190 doubles, 15 triples, and 59 home runs. Cerone also added 436 runs batted in to his career totals.

After retiring as a player, he worked in the business end of baseball and in 1998 founded the Newark Bears, an independent minor-league club, which competed in the Atlantic League.

In 2003, Cerone sold the team. Rick Cerone still resides in New Jersey with his family.

Rick Cerrone–Courtesy of Seton Hall University Athletic Communications

DERON L. CHERRY
Football
Riverside, New Jersey
Born: September 12, 1959

Deron Cherry was a tremendously talented athlete at Palmyra High School in Palmyra, New Jersey. After graduation, Deron decided to stay home in the Garden State, and Cherry picked Rutgers as his school of choice. At Rutgers, Deron Cherry starred for head coach Frank Burns during some of the state university's finest football years.

Deron was a strong safety and punter on a Rutgers squad that posted a 9–3 record in 1978. Rutgers went to its first bowl contest that season and lost to Arizona State (18–34) in the Garden State Bowl.

The following year, safety Deron Cherry had an enormously successful junior season. The defensive star helped lead Rutgers to eight wins against only three losses and excelled as the team's punter. Cherry averaged 41.3 yards per kick in 1979. For his superlative efforts as a pass defender and kicker, Deron was voted the team's Most Valuable Player and named to the All-East squad by the Associated Press (AP).

In 1980, senior Deron Cherry was voted defensive captain of the Scarlet Knights. His Scarlet squad recorded another winning season with seven victories and four defeats. Once again, Deron Cherry was voted team MVP and selected to the AP All-East squad. He also earned honorable mention All-America honors.

Deron Cherry concluded his outstanding Rutgers gridiron career with a total of nine interceptions. He punted 188 times while at Rutgers, for a total of 7,413 yards. Cherry had a career average of 39.4 yards per punt.

The NFL's Kansas City Chiefs signed Deron Cherry to a free-agent contract in 1981. After being one of the Chiefs' final cuts at the end of training camp, Deron rejoined the Kansas City club late in September of that same year.
Deron Cherry instantly developed into a key performer for the Chiefs and remained on the team as a starter for the next eleven years.

Cherry's uncanny ball-hawk instincts enabled him to consistently pick the pockets of would-be receivers. Deron made his first NFL interception against the Oakland Raiders in October of 1981. He added to his pass-pilfering resume game after game and season after season until it reached a remarkable total of fifty career interceptions.

Cherry's reputation as a vicious tackler was also easily documented. He had six 100-tackle seasons in his eleven years as a pro safety. Seven times over the span of his long and illustrious career, Deron Cherry was named to the All-Pro team (1983, 1984, 1985, 1986, 1987, 1988, 1989). In 1987, Cherry was selected as the Kansas City Chiefs' NFL Man of the Year. In 1988, Deron won the Byron White Humanitarian Award for service to his team, community, and country.

Deron Cherry remained active in civic and charitable organizations throughout his NFL career and his everyday life. In 1991, Cherry retired from pro football. In addition to his fifty pass interceptions, he also recovered fifteen fumbles during his career. He was named to the Kansas City Chiefs' Twenty-Five-Year All-Time Team and to the NFL's 1980s All-Decade Team.

Deron Cherry proved there is life after an athlete's playing days are over. He took on the world of business with the same gusto he used to intimidate pro pass receivers on the gridiron. In 1995, he became a limited-ownership partner in an NFL expansion team—the Jacksonville Jaguars. He is also involved in a number of other very successful business ventures. The fruits of Deron Cherry's athletic and business efforts have definitely produced abundant and well-deserved success for the ex-New Jersey and Kansas City star.

Deron Cherry–
Courtesy Kansas City
Chiefs Football

*Defensive star
Deron Cherry spent
his entire NFL
career with the
Kansas City Chiefs*

Deron Cherry–Courtesy Kansas City Chiefs Football

RON DAYNE
Football
Berlin, New Jersey
Born: March 14, 1978

He was known as "the Great Dayne" during his college football years at the University of Wisconsin. The exalted nickname was no exaggeration. Terrific tailback Ron Dayne set an astonishing NCAA record by rushing for over six thousand yards in his four-year career.

Ron Dayne was a two-sport star at Overbrook High School in Pine Hill, New Jersey. In addition to being a blue-chip football player, Dayne was also a track-and-field phenom with possible Olympic potential. In his junior year, Ron Dayne won the discus event at New Jersey's Track and Field Meet of Champions. As a senior, Dayne won New Jersey state titles in both the discus and shot-put events.

However, Ron Dayne turned his back on track and field to pursue a gridiron career. The five foot eleven inch, 250-pound-plus tailback accepted a football scholarship offer from coach Barry Alvarez to play running back for the University of Wisconsin. At Wisconsin, Dayne broke fast out of the starting gate. Ron gained an astounding 1,863 yards as a freshman runner. In the 1996 Copper Bowl, Ron gained 246 yards in leading Wisconsin to a 38–10 victory over Utah. For his efforts, Ron Dayne was named the Most Valuable Player of the Copper Bowl.

Dayne's yardage production dipped slightly as a sophomore. His total of 1,421 yards gained was still a stunning achievement for any runner. The Wisconsin Badgers played in the Outback Bowl that season, but were beaten by the Georgia Bulldogs 6–33.

As a junior, Ron Dayne gained 1,325 yards and helped carry the Badgers to a 38–31 victory over the UCLA Bruins in the Rose Bowl. Ron Dayne was named the game's MVP.

Wisconsin returned to the Rose Bowl to cap off Ron Dayne's stellar senior season. Dayne rushed for 1,834 yards in his final year as a college player. The Badgers also bested the Stanford Cardinals 17–9 in the Rose Bowl. Once again, tailback Ron Dayne was named the Rose Bowl's Most Valuable Player.

Ron Dayne was named an All-American in 1996, 1998, and 1999. In 1999, he won the Heisman Trophy as America's top college player. He also captured the Maxwell Award as college football's best player that same year.

The Great Dayne rushed for a grand total of 6,397 yards in regular-season play and tallied sixty-three touchdowns. Counting post-season bowl games, the Wisconsin star exploded on the gridiron for a stupendous total of 7,125 yards and seventy-one touchdowns. In all, twelve times as a Wisconsin Badger, Ron Dayne rushed for over two hundred yards in a game.

The New York Giants made Ron Dayne their first-round pick in the 2000 NFL draft. Dayne was the eleventh player selected overall. Ron Dayne was projected to be the perfect running mate for Giants' speedster Tiki Barber. However, the chemistry between their running styles was never quite right, and the high expectations for the terrific tandem fizzled out. The Giants did not re-sign Ron Dayne after the 2004 season. Dayne then signed and played with the Denver Broncos for a single season. The Houston Texans then added Ron Dayne to their stable of running backs for the 2006 season.

In 2007, Ron Dayne's Herculean rushing efforts in college were recognized by the University of Wisconsin with a fitting tribute. The Great Dayne's jersey number was permanently retired.

LAWRENCE EUGENE "LARRY" DOBY

Baseball
Paterson, New Jersey
Born: December 13, 1923

Larry Doby, like many other African o-American baseball stars of his day, began his professional career in the Negro Baseball Lleague. Doby was just seventeen years of age when he starred at second base for the Newark (N.J.) Eagles. He would later become a man who madke baseball history in the once all-white American League.

Lawrence Doby was born in Camden, South Carolina. However, he was raised in Paterson, New Jersey, where he grew to be a 6 six foot 1one inch, 180 - pound, naturally- gifted athlete. In his teens, he played pro baseball for the Newark Eagles under the assumed name of Larry Walker. Using the name Larry Walker helped the young infielder protect his amateur status from unwanted scrutiny. Doby began his career as a slick-fielding, soft-handed, second baseman, but was later shifted to center field, where he reigned as a ball hawk, blessed with blazing speed.

Doby's sports career was briefly curtailed by a two-year stint in the U.S. Navy. When he returned from military service in 1946, Larry teamed with fellow New Jersey Eagles' star Monte Irvin in leading their club to the championship of the Negro league.

Eleven weeks after Jackie Robinson broke the color barrier in the National League as a member of the Brooklyn Dodgers, Larry Doby was signed to a contract by Bill Veeck, the owner of the Cleveland Indians.

When Veeck met with the newest addition to his team, he told Doby, "You are going to be part of history."

Three hours after signing his contract, new Cleveland Indian Larry Doby pinch-hit for pitcher Bryan Stephens in a game against the Chicago White Sox in Comiskey Park. The date was July 5, 1947. Doby was retired on three strikes by White Sox hurler Earl Harris Larry Doby went down swinging, but struck a blow for equal rights during that plate appearance. Doby became the first black athlete to play baseball in the American League. Doby saw limited action that first season and appeared in only twenty-nine games.

The year 1948 was Larry Doby's first full year in the major leagues. Cleveland posted a season record of ninety-seven wins and fifty-eight losses to capture the

American League pennant. Doby hit .301 while collecting 132 hits in 439 at bats. He had twenty-three doubles, nine triples, and fourteen home runs. Larry also drove in sixty-six runs.

In the 1948 World Series against the Boston Braves, Doby banged out seven hits in twenty-two at bats to help the Indians best the Braves in six games. One of those hits was a sizzling shot over the fence in game four of the series.

The Indians added several other players of color to their roster in 1949. Larry Doby was joined by Luke Easer, Minnie Miñoso, and Satchel Paige. Doby banged out 152 hits that year, and among them were 25 doubles and 24 home runs. His total of eighty-five RBIs was tops on the team. He was named to the American League All-Star squad for the first time that season. Doby earned All-Star status every year from 1949 to 1955.

Yogi Berra, the perennial All-Star catcher from the New York Yankees had this to say about Larry Doby's skills as a player: "Larry Doby could do everything."

Doby upped his batting average to .326 in 1950. He drove in 102 runners and crushed 25 home runs. In 1951, the hard-hitting center fielder for the Tribe smashed twenty homers and had a .295 average.

The next year, Larry Doby exploded at the plate. He blasted thirty-two home runs to lead the American League in dingers. Doby also added 104 RBIs to his season total.

The lightning in Larry Doby's bat continued to shock opposing pitchers in 1953. He cracked 29 homers and collected 135 hits. He also totaled 102 runs batted in.

Doby's onslaught at the plate didn't let up. Larry led the American League with thirty-two home runs in 1954. He hit .272 and amassed 126 RBIs to top the league in that hitting category.

The Cleveland Indians won the American League pennant that season with a record of 111 wins and only 43 losses. The Indians faced the New York Giants in the World Series, and Larry Doby faced his old New Jersey pal and teammate from the Newark Eagles, Monte Irvin. The Giants bested the Indians in a four-game sweep of the series.

Larry Doby only hit .251 in 1955, but his batting totals included 143 hits, 75 RBIs, and 26 home runs. At the end of the season, the star outfielder was traded to the Chicago White Sox.

In Chicago, Doby teamed with Nellie Fox, Luis Aparicio, and Walt Dropo in leading the White Sox to a respectable season record of eighty-five wins and sixty-nine losses. Chicago finished in third place in the league behind the New York Yankees and the Cleveland Indians. Doby's contribution to the Sox success was 24 home runs and 102 runs batted in.

Larry Doby was thirty-three years old in 1957, but his age hardly slowed him down. He had 120 hits, including 14 home runs.

In 1958, it was back to the Tribe for Larry Doby. He returned to Cleveland and posted a .283 batting average.

Doby's last year in the major leagues was in 1959, when he split time with the Chicago White Sox and the Detroit Tigers. He played in twenty-one games for the Sox and eighteen games for the Tigers.

Larry Doby had a .283 career batting average. He had a total of 970 runs batted in and bashed 253 home runs. Doby played in 1,533 major-league games and hit at least twenty homers every year from 1949 to 1956.

In 1978, Larry Doby was hired to manage the Chicago White Sox. Doby became the second African American skipper in major-league history. (Frank Robinson of the Cleveland Indians became the first in 1975.) Doby guided the White Sox to a record of thirty-seven wins and eighty-seven losses before being replaced.

Larry Doby's number fourteen was retired by the Cleveland Indians in 1994. He was elected to the Baseball Hall of Fame in 1998.

Larry Doby, the baseball trailblazer, died in Montclair, New Jersey, on June 18, 2003. He was seventy-nine years old. On August 10, 2007, members of the Cleveland Indians team paid tribute to Larry Doby's enormous contributions to baseball and the world of sports by wearing his number fourteen on their uniforms.

Hall of Fame pitcher Bob Feller had this to say about Larry Doby: "He was a great guy, a great center fielder, and a great teammate," said Feller after Doby's passing.

ANNE DONOVAN
Basketball
Ridgewood, New Jersey
Born: November 1, 1961

She was the first winner of the Champion Player of the Year Award presented by the Women's Basketball Coaches Association. She was the first female sports star to play on a college national championship team and then to coach a team to a professional title. She was the first woman coach to capture a WNBA crown. When it comes to groundbreaking accomplishments in women's basketball, New Jersey's Anne Donovan is the name that first comes to mind. The gifted six foot eight inch center is one of the game's all-time greats.

Anne Donovan was born in Ridgewood, New Jersey, and starred on the court for Paramus Catholic High School in Paramus, New Jersey. As a senior, Anne was the most sought-after female basketball player in the country. She decided to attend Old Dominion University in Virginia. Old Dominion is one of the top ten women's basketball teams in all-time winning percentage. Anne Donovan was slated to fill the shoes of another great women's basketball superstar, Nancy Lieberman. Lieberman graduated after winning women's basketball's coveted Wade Trophy two years in a row.

Anne Donovan was not only up to the tough task of replacing one of the game's all-time greats, she promptly carved her own immortal niche in the annals of women's hoop history. She played all 136 games scheduled by Old Dominion during her four-year college career. Anne helped lead the Lady Monarchs to a national championship in 1980. Old Dominion defeated the University of Tennessee 68–53 to capture the Association of Intercollegiate Athletics for Women (AIAW) (large college) tournament crown. The AIAW was later replaced by the current NCAA Women's Championship Tournament. With Anne Donovan in the middle of the Lady Monarchs' offense and defense, Old Dominion was ranked in the top ten of the AP's Final Women's Basketball Poll all four years of Anne's reign.

In 1983, senior Anne Donovan became the very first female winner of the Naismith College Player of the Year Award. She was also honored as the Player of the Year by the Women's Basketball Coaches Association and presented with the Broderick Award as the college woman athlete of the year. She added All-America basketball honors to her sports resume for the third year in a row.

During her phenomenal four-year college career, Anne Donovan scored 2,719 points and ripped off 1,976 rebounds. Donovan also blocked 801 shots. Amazingly, Anne averaged a double-double for her entire career at Old Dominion. She averaged twenty points and 14.5 rebounds per game over a four-year span.

Anne Donovan was a member of the 1980 U.S. Women's Olympic Basketball Team, but missed playing in the games because of the U.S. boycott of the Moscow Olympics. In 1984, Donovan was on the United States Olympic squad that won a gold medal in the Los Angeles Games. She repeated her gold-medal win in the 1988 Olympic Games in Seoul, South Korea.

Unfortunately, opportunities to play women's professional basketball in the U.S. before the arrival of the WNBA (in 1996-97) were few. Anne Donovan played pro ball in Japan and Italy from 1983 to 1989.

At the conclusion of the 1989 season, Donovan retired as a player and moved to the sidelines as a coach and hoops mentor. She coached at Old Dominion from 1989 to 1995 and at East Carolina University from 1995 to 1997. Donovan then took her vast court knowledge to the professional ranks. She coached the Philadelphia Rage in the American Basketball League until the league folded. Anne then skippered the WNBA's Indiana Fever for the 2000 season.

In 2001, Anne Donovan jumped to the Charlotte Sting and guided the North Carolina club to the finals of the WNBA tourney. The Sting lost to the Los Angeles Sparks coached by Michael Cooper in the finals. Donovan stayed with Charlotte until 2003, when she became the head coach of the Seattle Storm. In 2004, Anne Donovan captured lightning in a bottle, and the Seattle Storm won the WNBA Championship.

Anne Donovan added to her Olympic gold collection in 2004 when the U.S. team finished first in Athens, Greece. Donovan was an assistant coach, along with Rutgers's C. Vivian Stringer on a staff headed by Van Chancellor of the WNBA's Houston Comets.

In 2006, Anne Donovan was named the head coach of the 2008 Women's Olympic Basketball Team. In 2007, Anne resigned as the head coach of the Seattle Storm.

Anne Donovan is a member of the Basketball Hall of Fame and will always be remembered as one of the game's first and foremost all-time greats.

Anne Donovan–Courtesy NBAE Getty Images/Seattle Supersonics & Storm

JAMES THOMAS DOWD
Ice Hockey
Brick, New Jersey
Born: December 25, 1968

It's one of those great sports stories everyone loves to hear or read about. Jim Dowd is New Jersey's version of the local hockey hero who made it big in pro sports and eventually won a coveted championship title. How many young, ice hockey stars in the Garden State aspire to a successful career in the National Hockey League? How many youthful skaters dream about winning Stanley Cup championships? How many New Jersey ice athletes fantasize about hoisting the magnificent Stanley Cup in the air and taking a victory lap as a member of their home state's pro-hockey club? All of those amazing elements are true parts of Jim Dowd's life on the ice as an NHL star.

Center Jim Dowd helped the New Jersey Devils capture the NHL's prized Stanley Cup in 1995.

Jim Dowd was a standout center on the Brick Township High School hockey team in the mid-1980s. The six foot one inch, 190-pound middleman on the ice led Brick Township to the New Jersey Interscholastic Athletic Association ice hockey title in 1985–86. Dowd was a sharp puck handler with good speed and a rocket shot. Jim racked up a total of 375 points during his four-year high school career to set a New Jersey state record. He blasted home 189 goals and served up 186 assists as a high school player.

Jim Dowd's astonishing on-ice accomplishments did not go unnoticed by pro scouts, even though the Garden State is not considered a hotbed for hockey prospects. Dowd was the eighth-round selection of the New Jersey Devils in the 1987 NHL entry draft. Jim was the 149th player picked overall.

Jim Dowd decided to enroll at Lake Superior State University, a school with a rich college hockey tradition. In 1990, Dowd was an NCAA West Second Team All-American and a Central Collegiate Hockey Association Second Team All-American. The following year, Jim Dowd was a First Team All-America choice. He was also the Central Collegiate Hockey Association's Player of the Year in 1991.

Over the course of his four-year career at Lake Superior State University, Dowd tallied a grand total of 274 points. He netted 91 goals and collected 183 assists.

After college, Jim Dowd turned pro. He first paid some hockey dues with a short stint in the American Hockey League (AHL) as a member of the minor-league Utica Devils. He later stepped up to the parent club and played a single game for the New Jersey Devils in 1991–92. Dowd was the first New Jersey native to ever don a Devils' uniform in an NHL game. After his short-lived NHL debut, Dowd returned to the AHL, where he excelled as a top scorer for the Albany River Rats.

The Devils used Dowd on the big-time ice occasionally, and he yo-yoed between the AHL and the NHL in 1993–94. However, Jim's brief appearances in National Hockey League contests were extremely productive. He scored five goals and added ten assists in just fifteen regular-season games.

In 1994–95, a shoulder injury, and a league labor dispute, which shortened the NHL season, hampered Dowd's pro progress. Nevertheless, Jim Dowd was a member of the New Jersey Devils club, which defeated the Detroit Red Wings in the Stanley Cup finals. In fact, center Jim Dowd blasted the game-winning goal in game two of the Stanley Cup Play-offs. The homegrown hero became a Stanley Cup Champion playing for his home-state team.

Center Jim Dowd began a long and distinguished pro hockey career, playing for numerous teams. He played for the Vancouver Canucks in 1995 and briefly for the New York Islanders in 1996. Dowd was on the Calgary Flame in 1997 and was a middleman for the Edmonton Oilers in 1998 and 1999.

When the Minnesota Wild joined the NHL in 2000 as an expansion team, they made Jim Dowd part of their team plan. Dowd skated for Minnesota from 2000 to 2004 and appeared in a total of 283 games. He scored a total of 121 points on 32 goals, coupled with 89 assists for Minnesota.

Jim Dowd traveled north to play for the Montreal Canadians in 2003–04 and flew into the Windy City for a stay with the Chicago Black Hawks in 2005–06. The former Brick Township star spent a season with the Colorado Avalanche in 2005–06 before rejoining the New Jersey Devils in 2006–07. The well-traveled Dowd, who skated around the NHL, had played in over 650 pro games by the 2007–08 season. Jim Dowd will best be remembered as the hometown hockey hero who grew up in the Garden State and eventually won a Stanley Cup Championship as a member of the New Jersey Devils.

Jim Dowd–Courtesy Lake Superior State University

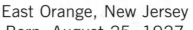

ALTHEA GIBSON
Tennis
East Orange, New Jersey
Born: August 25, 1927

"I always wanted to be somebody," was the credo of tennis icon Althea Gibson. Gibson was a product of poverty and humble beginnings. As a child, Althea seemed a most unlikely choice for eventual sports immortality. However, Althea Gibson did for tennis what Jackie Robinson did for major-league baseball. Althea Gibson broke the unspoken racial barrier that barred black athletes from participating in tennis's top tournaments.

Althea Gibson was a true tennis trailblazer. She was the first black athlete to compete in the U.S. Open Tennis Championship. Gibson was the first black athlete to compete in the Wimbledon Tennis Tournament. Later in life, she was New Jersey's first black female athletics commissioner.

Althea Gibson more than achieved her goal to be somebody. Indeed, she was somebody special. She was a fearless sports pioneer, an advocate of civil rights, and perhaps most of all, Althea Gibson was a great athlete and tennis player. Althea Gibson was born in a cabin on a cotton farm in the tiny town of Silver, South Carolina. She was the oldest of four children. Her parents were sharecroppers who struggled to feed their family. Althea was sent to live with her aunt in Harlem, New York. Althea became a tough street kid who was good at all sports. By the time Althea's family moved to Harlem, and the Gibsons were reunited, she was already an expert at stickball, basketball, and paddle tennis.

Althea had a natural talent for the game of paddle tennis. She won the Paddle Championship of New York City in 1939. It wasn't long before Althea graduated to the game of lawn tennis. Friends and mentors helped Althea join the Cosmopolitan Tennis Club in Harlem, where she practiced with resident pros who encouraged her. Gibson needed little encouragement, for she was fiercely determined to succeed. In 1942, Althea Gibson played in her first tennis tournament. She won the Girls' Singles Championship in the New York State Open Tennis Tournament for black players. At the time, black tennis players were not allowed to compete against white players. Althea Gibson was fifteen years old when she won her first tournament.

Althea began playing in all-black American Tennis Association tournaments. Eventually, Gibson won ten straight women's singles titles. In 1949, three years after Jackie Robinson broke the color barrier in baseball, Althea Gibson splintered the barrier that separated black and white athletes in tennis. Althea became the first black tennis star to participate in the National Indoor Tournament. (She was also playing college tennis for Florida A & M University at the time.) Gibson finished second in the National Indoor Tournament, which entitled her to compete in the U.S. National at Forest Hills (the forerunner of the U.S. Open Tennis Championship. Of course, a black athlete participating in the U.S. National at Forest Hills was unheard of at that time. Gibson was not extended an invitation to participate.

Alice Marble, a famous white tennis star, was deeply offended by the snub of Althea and personally championed Gibson's cause. Marble wrote a moving letter of support to a national tennis magazine. The letter created a public controversy. Tennis officials were shamed into inviting Althea Gibson to play in the 1950 U.S. National at Forest Hills. The race barrier in tennis was finally shattered once and for all. A year later, Althea Gibson became the first black tennis player to compete at Wimbledon. In 1952, Althea Gibson was the ninth-ranked player in the United States Lawn Tennis Association standings.

The doors to major tournaments were suddenly opening, but Althea Gibson had difficulty elevating her caliber of play. She was frustrated by her lack of success and for a short period considered quitting tennis.

However, Gibson's slight slump leveled out in 1956, and she resumed her usual winning ways. Althea won the French Singles Championship and the Italian Singles Championship. She paired with Angela Buxton to capture doubles titles at Wimbledon and at the French Championships. In 1956, Althea Gibson became the first African American to ever win a Grand Slam event.

In 1957, Althea Gibson played her heart out and won everlasting fame as one of tennis's all-time greats. She became the first African American player to win a singles championship at Wimbledon. She became the first African American star to capture the U.S. Open singles crown. Althea Gibson also won the doubles title at Wimbledon with Darlene Hard and the U.S. mixed doubles title with Kurt Nielsen. She added a National Clay Court Championship and an Australian doubles title. It was an astounding year of achievements for Althea Gibson. It was topped off when Gibson was voted the Associated Press Female Athlete of the Year. No woman sports figure of African American descent had ever been so honored.

Althea continued on her winning rampage in 1958. She repeated as the Wimbledon Singles Champion. Gibson added her second straight U.S. Open Singles title. The team of Althea Gibson and Maria Bueno captured the women's doubles title at Wimbledon that same year.

After Althea Gibson won all there was to win as an amateur in tennis, she found herself without a means of support. There was no pro tennis circuit or prize money available. Product endorsements were few and far between for the amazing star who'd won eleven Grand Slam victories.

Althea Gibson signed a contract to play tennis exhibitions during halftime of Harlem Globetrotter basketball games. She also embarked upon a singing career and penned her famous autobiography, entitled, *I Always Wanted To Be Somebody*. Althea Gibson tried her hand at golf and in 1963 became the first African American woman on the Ladies' Professional Golf Association (LPGA) tour.

Althea Gibson lived in New Jersey for many years. She coached youth tennis in East Orange, New Jersey, which is the home of the Althea Gibson Early Childhood Academy, a public elementary school. In 1975, she became State Commissioner of Athletics in New Jersey and held the position for ten years. Gibson also served on the New Jersey State Athletics Control Board until 1988 and on the Governor's Council on Physical Fitness until 1992.

Althea Gibson, along with her longtime friend, Frances Gray, cofounded the Althea Gibson Foundation, dedicated to providing educational opportunities to youth through athletics.

Althea Gibson died in East Orange, New Jersey, on September 28, 2003. She was seventy-six years old. Althea Gibson never thought of herself as a sports pioneer or civil-rights trailblazer. "Her contribution to the civil rights movement was done with her tennis racket," Ms. Gray once commented.

Althea Gibson has been inducted into the International Tennis Hall of Fame and the International Women's Sports Hall of Fame.

Althea Gibson–Courtesy Florida A & M University Sports Information/Media

LEON ALLEN "GOOSE" GOSLIN
Baseball
Salem, New Jersey
Born: October 16, 1900

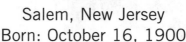

The way he handled a bat made him the mortal enemy of most opposing pitchers. Fly balls were his enemy, and the way he shagged them in the outfield drove his teammates batty. As he circled under a fly ball, Leon Goslin would frantically wave his arms like a big bird flapping its wings during takeoff. That is how Leon Goslin became known as "Goose" Goslin forevermore.

Goose Goslin played during the heyday of major-league baseball. He took the field against diamond icons like Babe Ruth, Lou Gehrig, Ty Cobb, Tris Speaker, Jimmie Foxx, and others. Goslin's name deserves to be mentioned with the greatest players the game has ever known. The Goose wasn't graceful when camping under deep fly balls, but Goslin knew how to play the game of baseball, and he played it extremely well.

Leon "Goose" Goslin was born in Salem, New Jersey, and left home at the age of sixteen to play semipro baseball along the East Coast. Goose was a left-handed contact hitter who put the bat on the ball often and with authority. Goose doubled as a pitcher, and by the age of nineteen was playing minor-league baseball.

The old Washington Senators called twenty-year-old Goose Goslin up to the major leagues late in 1921. Goose collected thirteen hits in fifty at bats, including a double, a triple, and a towering home run. In 1922, Goose Goslin became the Washington Senators' regular left fielder. In 1922, Goslin amassed 116 hits and had a .324 batting average.

In 1923, Goose posted a .300 batting average. His 180 hits included 29 doubles, 18 triples, and 9 home runs. The Goose's big bat was one reason why the Washington Senators won the American League pennant in 1924. Another reason the Senators captured the crown was Washington pitcher Walter Johnson, who won twenty-three games that season and posted a 2.72 earned run average. When all was said and done, in 1924, Johnson's major-league mound wins would total 373 victories. The Senators went on to beat the New York Giants four games to three games in the 1924 World Series. Goslin had three home runs and seven runs batted in against the Giants.

The Senators won the American League pennant for a second straight time in 1925. Goose Goslin had another superlative season. Goose banged out 201 hits.

He led the American League with twenty triples and also crashed eighteen home runs. His .334 batting average was second best among the Senators' starters (Sam Rice hit .350). In the 1925 World Series, the Pittsburgh Pirates, led by the phenomenal Pie Traynor, beat the Senators four games to three games. Goslin hit .308 in the series, and blasted three home runs.

Goose continued to pick on opposing pitchers for the next three years. He blasted 201 hits in 1926 and had a .354 batting average. Goslin put up strong numbers at the plate again in 1927. He had a .334 batting average and collected 194 hits.

The Goose leveled the lumber and really rocked opposing hurlers in 1928. All through the 1928 season, Goose Goslin battled Heinie Manush of the Saint Louis Browns for the American League batting title. In his final at bat in the last game of the season, Goose smashed a hit to capture the AL batting crown. Heinie Manush batted .378 in 1928. Goose Goslin batted .379 to top the league in average.

Goslin's methodic hitting fell off for the first time in his career after he won the American League batting championship. He hit .288 in 1929 and was hitting .271 for the Senators in 1930 when he was sent to the Saint Louis Browns.

The move to Saint Louis revived Goslin's murderous swing. He hit .320 and bashed 129 hits for the Browns. Numbered among those hits was a career-high thirty home runs. Goslin hit three home runs in a game against the Philadelphia Athletics on August 19, 1930.

In 1931, Goose Goslin put up some serious numbers at the plate. He collected 194 hits, which included 42 doubles, 10 triples, and 24 home runs. His batting average was a hefty .328. Goose's RBI total was 105. In his first two years in Saint Louis, Goose Goslin blasted 54 homers and drove in 205 runs.

In 1932, Goslin's average dipped to .299, but he still racked up 171 hits with 28 doubles, 9 triples, and 17 home runs. Goose' s bat also sent 104 runners across the plate for the Browns. He drove in one hundred or more runs for a third straight year in Saint Louis.

Goose Goslin migrated back to Washington for the 1933 season. The Senators won the AL pennant and then lost to the New York Giants four games to one game in the World Series. Goslin hit .297 with ten home runs during the regular season. He batted .250 in the World Series. Once again, the Senators decided to trade the Goose. They sent Goslin to the Detroit Tigers, where he joined forces with Hank Greenberg, Charles Gehringer, and Mickey Cochrane.

The Tigers roared their way to the American League pennant with some help from Goose Goslin, who hit .305 that season. The Tigers took on the Saint Louis Cardinals' Gas House Gang of Pepper Martin, Frankie Frisch, and New Jersey native Joe "Ducky" Medwick. The Cardinals topped the Tigers four games to three games to win the championship.

Detroit repeated as American League Champions in 1935. Goslin hit .292 by bashing 172 hits. In the World Series, the Detroit Tigers ripped the Chicago Cubs four games to two games to earn the major-league baseball crown. Goose Goslin drove home the winning run for Detroit in game six to ice the title for the Tigers.

Goose stayed with the Tigers for two more seasons. He hit .315 in 1936 and crushed twenty-four home runs. However, in 1937, Goose Goslin finally began to slow down at the plate. He played in only seventy-nine games and hit .238. The Tigers released Goose after the 1937 season, and he was signed by his old team, the Washington Senators.

The year 1938 was Goose Goslin's final year in the big leagues as a player. He played in only thirty-seven games and managed only nine hits in fifty-seven at bats.

Goose Goslin played eighteen years in the major leagues. Goose Goslin played in 2,287 games and posted a .316 career batting average. Goslin cracked 2,735 hits. Of his 921 extra-base hits, 500 were doubles, 173 were triples, and 248 were home runs. Goose had 1,609 RBIs and scored 1,483 runs. Three times in his career he hit three home runs in a single game. Goose had a twenty-five-game hitting streak in 1928 and a thirty-game hitting streak in 1934. He had four hits, including a home run, in game four of the 1924 World Series against the New York Giants.

In 1968, Goose Goslin was inducted into the Baseball Hall of Fame. At the ceremony, Goslin said, "I want to thank God, who gave me the health and strength to compete with these great players. I will never forget this. I will take this to my grave."

Leon Allen "Goose" Goslin passed away May 15, 1971, at seventy-one years of age.

FRANCO HARRIS
Football
Fort Dix, New Jersey
Born: March 7, 1950

Penn State football coach Joe Paterno used him mostly as a blocking back for Nittany Lions' star tailback Lydell Mitchell. Pro-football fans were shocked when the Pittsburgh Steelers bypassed Lydell Mitchell and made Franco Harris their first-round draft pick in the 1972 NFL draft. Lydell Mitchell was a later pick in the draft and did go on to have a fine pro career with the Baltimore (now Indianapolis) Colts. However, it was former blocker Franco Harris's star that shined the brightest as a pro performer in the National Football League (NFL).

Franco Harris was born in Fort Dix, but played high school football at Rancocas Valley Regional High School in Mount Holly, New Jersey. As a junior, Harris was a member of a New Jersey All-State gridiron squad that included quarterback Joe Theismann (South River) and running back Jack Tatum (Passaic). All three later distinguished themselves as NFL stars.

After graduation, Franco Harris attended Pennsylvania State University, where he was paired with another New Jersey native, Lydell Mitchell (Salem). Together, Harris and Mitchell formed one of the most dynamic backfield duos in Penn State football history. Franco Harris mainly blasted holes open as a hard-hitting lead blocker. Fleet-footed Lydell Mitchell responded by scoring twenty-nine touchdowns in 1971.

It was Mitchell's collegiate scoring resume that made him more appealing to pro-football fans. However, the Pittsburgh Steelers knew what they were doing when they made Franco Harris the thirteenth player selected in the 1972 draft. Harris had rushed for over two thousand yards and scored twenty-four touchdowns in college.

Franco Harris wasted no time in establishing himself as a ground-gaining force in the NFL. His first year as a pro quickly won over Steeler fans who had questioned his ability to tote the pigskin. Harris gained 1,055 yards on 188 carries for an average of 5.6 yards per carry. Franco also racked up ten touchdowns and reeled in three touchdown passes. Franco Harris became an instant scoring sensation and a fantastic fan favorite especially with Pittsburgh's large Italian-American population. Franco's mother is Italian and his father is African American.

In 1972, Franco Harris took part in one of the most famous plays in the history of the National Football League. The play was dubbed "the Immaculate Reception" by Pittsburgh sportscaster Myron Cope. It has been known as such ever since. The Immaculate Reception occurred in a play-off contest between the Pittsburgh Steelers and the Oakland Raiders. The Raiders were clinging to a slim 7–6 lead with only twenty-two seconds left in the game. The Steelers had the ball. Quarterback Terry Bradshaw fired a desperation pass to Pittsburgh's John "Frenchy" Fuqua as Raiders' safety Jack Tatum zeroed in to make the hit. The ball bounced away from both players and seemed to be headed to the turf, where it would be ruled incomplete. Pittsburgh's Franco Harris, who was trailing the play at full speed, raced toward the ball and scooped it into his hands just barely before it hit the ground. Harris stumbled forward with the pigskin clutched in his mitts, regained his balance, and sped into the end zone. Harris scored the game-winning touchdown with only seconds remaining. The Immaculate Reception instantly became part of pro-football folklore.

Franco Harris was rewarded for his first fabulous season as a pro by being named the league's Offensive Rookie of the Year by United Press International, the Associated Press, and the *Sporting News*. He was also chosen to play in the Pro Bowl. It was Franco's first of nine straight Pro Bowl selections.

The Pittsburgh Steelers won seven AFC Central Division titles from 1972 to 1979. They also captured four AFC Championships (1974, 1975, 1978, and 1979).

In 1974, the Pittsburgh Steelers topped the Minnesota Vikings by the score of 16–6 in Super Bowl IX (played January 12, 1975). Franco Harris was named the game's Most Valuable Player. In the contest, Harris gained 158 yards in thirty-four carries and scored one touchdown.

Franco Harris had an outstanding season in 1975. He rushed for 1,246 yards to set a Steelers' record. The Pittsburgh Steelers also won their second Super Bowl, besting the tough Dallas Cowboys 21–26.

The 1976 season proved to be fruitful for Franco Harris. He found the end zone on numerous occasions and tallied fourteen touchdowns.

Running back Franco Harris was picked All-Pro in 1977. In 1978, Harris and his Steeler teammates, including quarterback Terry Bradshaw, wide receiver Lynn Swann, and linebacker Jack Lambert, returned to the Super Bowl and were once again matched against the formidable Dallas Cowboys. The Cowboys were led by quarterback Roger Staubach, running back Tony Dorsett, and wide receiver Drew

Pearson. Prior to the kickoff, Franco Harris made his feelings about the much-publicized rematch known to the press. "You either win or lose," said Franco Harris, "and I don't like to be a loser." Franco Harris and the Pittsburgh Steelers emerged from Super Bowl XIII victorious. The Steelers edged the Cowboys 35–31.

The fourth and final Super Bowl victory of Franco Harris's career came in the 1979 season. The Pittsburgh Steelers defeated the Los Angeles Rams 31–19 in Super Bowl XIV. Franco rushed for 1,186 yards that season. It was the seventh time in his career that Harris had rushed for over one thousand yards in an NFL season.

Franco Harris was a member of the Pittsburgh Steelers until 1983 and played his final year in the NFL with the Seattle Seahawks (1984). In his thirteen professional seasons, Harris gained 12,120 yards on 2,949 carries, for a 4.1 yard per carry average. He scored a total of ninety-one rushing touchdowns. Franco also grabbed 307 passes for 2,287 yards and nine touchdowns. Franco Harris was named to the NFL 1970s All-Decade Team. He was inducted into the Pro Football Hall of Fame in 1990.

THOMAS WILLIAM HEINSOHN
Basketball
Jersey City, New Jersey
Born: August 26, 1934

Tommy Heinsohn is one of New Jersey's first pro-basketball superstars. Heinsohn played on eight NBA Championship teams with the Boston Celtics and later coached two Celtic clubs to NBA crowns. The six foot seven inch Jersey City native was born to be basketball royalty.

Tommy Heinsohn's reign as a king of the hoop court began at St. Michael's High School in Jersey City, New Jersey. Heinsohn was an all-around center who could control the tempo of a game at both ends of the court. His natural ability and size attracted a lot of attention from college recruiters.

Tommy accepted a scholarship to play basketball at College of the Holy Cross in Massachusetts. Heinsohn developed a unique line-drive hook shot, which seemed to be radar guided. It was tough to defend and exciting to see executed. The big man from Jersey City starred at Holy Cross from 1953 to 1956, and shined in the national spotlight on several occasions. He once scored fifty-one points in a game against the Boston College Eagles. In 1956, Heinsohn led Holy Cross to a record of twenty-two wins (22–4 overall) and a number-fourteen ranking in the Associated Press National Basketball Poll. Heinsohn was named to the All-America squad his senior year, when he scored a total of 700 points and averaged 27.4 points per game.

Over his three-year career at Holy Cross, Tommy Heinsohn hammered home 1,789 career points and averaged 22.7 points per college hoop contest.

Tom Heinsohn was signed by the Boston Celtics after graduation. In Boston, he joined forces with rebounding phenom Bill Russell and guard whiz Bob Cousy, another former Holy Cross graduate. Together, the threesome formed the nucleus of a rising NBA dynasty orchestrated by that great court conductor, coach Red Auerbach.

In 1956–57, Tommy Heinsohn was switched from center to forward and rapidly developed a line-drive jump shot to go along with his famous line-drive hook shot. Heinsohn racked up 16.2 points per game in his first pro season and wrestled down 705 rebounds. For his awesome debut season in the NBA, Heinsohn was named the league's Rookie of the Year. He was also voted to the All-Star squad. Tommy Heinsohn's teammate Bob Cousy was voted the league's Most

Valuable Player. To top things off, the Boston Celtics beat the Saint Louis Hawks four games to three games in the play-offs to capture the 1957 NBA Championship.

In Tommy Heinsohn's nine seasons as a player with Boston, the super Celtics won eight NBA crowns. The Boston Celtics won championships from 1959 to 1965. (The Hawks avenged their 1957 loss by topping the Celtics four games to three games in the 1958 play-off finals.) Heinsohn's best year individually was 1961–62, when he averaged 22.3 points per game.

Hampered by injuries late in his career, Heinsohn retired after the 1964–65 season. Tommy scored a total of 12,194 points as an NBA player. He averaged 18.6 points per game over his career and ripped down 5,749 rebounds. In 104 play-off contests, Tom Heinsohn added 2,058 points for a 19.8 per game average.

Tommy Heinsohn stepped off the basketball court in 1965, but returned to the NBA sidelines in 1969. Heinsohn was named the head coach of the Boston Celtics. In 1973, coach Tom Heinsohn guided the Celtics to an amazing league record of sixty-eight wins and only fourteen losses. It was the best record ever posted in Boston Celtic history. Heinsohn was named the NBA Coach of the Year.

In 1974, the Celtics won fifty-six games and lost twenty-six. With help from star players Dave Cowens, Jo Jo White, Paul Silas, and John "Hondo" Havlicek, the Cetics added the 1974 NBA Championship to Coach Heinsohn's list of accomplishments. Boston topped the Milwaukee Bucks four games to three games in the championship series.

Coach Tom Heinsohn garnered another championship gem for his cache of NBA crown jewels in 1976. The Celtics posted a season record of fifty-four wins and twenty-eight losses and went on to beat the Phoenix Suns four games to two in the NBA Championship Series. Boston's Jo Jo White was the Most Valuable Player of the title series.

Tom Heinsohn retired from coaching after the 1977–78 season. He won 427 games and lost 263 contests as a NBA coach.

Tommy Heinsohn's number fifteen has been retired by the Boston Celtics. He worked as a color commentator for NBA television broadcasts in the 1980s. Tommy Heinsohn was inducted into the Basketball Hall of Fame as a player in 1986.

All American Tom Heinsohn averaged 27.4 points per game as a center at Holy Cross in 1955-56

Thomas William (Tom) Heisohn–Courtesy of College of the Holy Cross, Sports Information & Sports Media

OREL LEONARD HERSHISER

Baseball
Cherry Hill, New Jersey
Born: September 16, 1958

Tommy LaSorda, the famous manager of the Los Angeles Dodgers, dubbed him, "the Bulldog" because Orel Hershiser was fiercely tenacious on the pitching mound. Orel was a never-quit kind of guy who didn't have overpowering speed or stupefying stuff as a hurler. Orel Hershiser was a shrewd and crafty mound magician. He had four good pitches, a sinking fastball, a slider, a deceptive curve, and a changeup. They were good, but not great pitches. The thing that made Orel Hirshiser a great pitcher was his uncanny ability to know when to throw just the right pitch at the right time. The Bulldog barked perfect pitches at big-league batters, and more often than not denied them advancement onto the base paths.

Orel Leonard Hershiser was born in Buffalo, New York, but spent his youth in Cherry Hill, New Jersey. He attended Cherry Hill High School East, where he was a star pitcher. After he graduated from high school, Orel attended Bowling Green State University in Ohio. It was at Bowling Green State that major-league scouts first noticed and appreciated the diamond talents of the young, right-handed hurler.

Orel Hershiser was drafted in the seventeenth round of the 1979 amateur baseball draft by the Los Angeles Dodgers. Hershiser spent a number of years in the minor leagues, sharpening his skills and gritting his teeth as he anxiously waited for a call up to the big time. Finally, the call came from the Los Angeles Dodgers on September 1,1983. The Bulldog began his major-league career in the pen as a middle reliever. In 1984, Orel posted a record of eleven wins and eight losses with a 2.66 earned run average. He also counted four shutouts among his eight victories. His stats were good enough to elevate him to a starting spot on the Dodgers' pitching rotation.

The Bulldog really roared in 1985, as Hershiser snapped off win after win. Orel's record was a stunning 19–3 that season, with an amazing 2.03 earned run average. Hershiser's phenomenal year in 1985 was difficult to duplicate, and the Bulldog recorded a 14–14 mark in 1986.

In 1987, the Dodgers' star pitcher won sixteen games and lost sixteen games, while posting a 3.06 earned run average. Hershiser was named to the National League All-Star squad that same season.

Orel Hershiser experienced a once-in-a-lifetime season in 1988. The Bulldog chewed up opposing batters to garner a mound mark of twenty-three wins and eight losses. He led the league by pitching fifteen complete games. He ended the season by pitching a record fifty-nine consecutive scoreless innings. His earned run average was a meager 2.26. He led the league in shutouts with 8, and also in innings pitched, with 267.

In the 1988 National League Championship Series (NLCS), the Los Angeles Dodgers faced off against the New York Mets. Hershiser started games one and three and picked up a save in game four. In game seven, Orel pitched a shutout win to give the Dodgers a four-games-to-three-games victory over manager Davey Johnson's Mets. Orel Hershiser was named the Most Valuable Player of the NLCS.

In the World Series against manager Tony La Russa's Oakland A's, the Bulldog hurler earned a complete game shutout to win in game two and a complete game victory in game five. The Dodgers captured the World Series crown, winning four of five contests against Oakland. Once again, Orel Hershiser was anointed for his diamond accomplishments. Hershiser was voted the MVP of the 1988 World Series.

The awards continued to pour in for Orel Hershiser in 1988. He was present-ed with a Gold Glove Award. He captured the prestigious Cy Young Award. Orel was named the Sporting News Pitcher of the Year, and he was voted the Male Athlete of the Year by the Associated Press.

It would be almost impossible for any pitcher to ever duplicate the kind of year Orel Hershiser had in 1988. He is the only player to win the Cy Young Award, the NLCS Most Valuable Player Award, and the World Series Most Valuable Player Award all in the same season.

In 1989, Hershiser went 15–15 on the mound, but had a great 2.31 earned run average. As a team, the Dodgers had an anemic offensive output in 1989, which hurt Hershiser's won-lost record.

In 1990, Orel Hershiser suffered an injury that threatened to end his brilliant career. He tore a rotator cuff in his pitching arm, which waylaid the Bulldog for over a year. He returned in 1991 to post a seven and two record on the mound for the Dodgers. Orel Hershiser remained a mainstay in the Dodgers pitching rota-tion until 1995, when he jumped leagues and joined the Cleveland Indians.

The Bulldog's bite was back in 1995. Hershiser used his old mound magic to baffle American League batters, and he ended up winning sixteen games while losing just six games. His work on the hill was a key factor in getting the Cleveland Indians into the American League Championship Series (ALCS). Manager Mike Hargrove's Indians dominated the Seattle Mariners, managed by Lou Piniella, and won the series four games to two games. Pitcher Orel Hershiser was named the Most Valuable Player of the ALCS to become the first person ever to capture MVP awards in both the NLCS and the ALCS.

In the World Series, the Indians were defeated by the Atlanta Braves, managed by Bobby Cox, in six games.

Hershiser pitched for two more seasons in Cleveland and was 14–6 for the Indians in 1997 when the Tribe captured the American League pennant. The Indians lost to the Florida Marlins in a tough seven-game World Series to end the year in baseball.

The year 1997 was also Orel Hershiser's last year in Cleveland. The Bulldog pitched for the San Francisco Giants in 1998. He became a New York Met in 1999. On July 22, 1999, while pitching for the Mets, Orel Hershiser got his two hundredth career win. It was a 7–4 victory over the Montreal Expos. On October 3,1999, the Bulldog recorded the two thousandth strikeout of his career. The victim was Melvin Mora of the Pittsburgh Pirates. Hershiser appeared in thirty-two games as a New York Met in 1999. He won thirteen games and lost twelve games.

Orel Hershiser, the pitcher known as the Bulldog, rejoined the Los Angeles Dodgers in 2000 for his final major-league season. His regular-season career stats are impressive. Hershiser won 204 games and lost 149 games on the mound. His career ERA was 3.48. The Bulldog also chalked up 2,014 strikeouts.

After his retirement as a player, Orel Hershiser worked as a major-league pitching coach and a TV analyst of major-league baseball games.

Orel Hershiser–Courtesy Los Angeles Dodgers

Orel Hershiser was the Associated Press Male Athlete of the Year in 1988

Orel Hershiser–Courtesy Los Angeles Dodgers

Orel Hershiser pitched 59 consecutive scoreless innings during the 1988 season

Orel Hershiser–Courtesy Los Angeles Dodgers

MONTFORD MERRILL "MONTE" IRVIN

Baseball
Orange, New Jersey
Born: February 25, 1919

The teams had names like the New York Black Yankees, the Kansas City Monarchs, and the Birmingham Black Barons. They were professional baseball clubs in the Negro Baseball League. It was a sad chapter in American sports history. African American athletes were denied the right to participate in the top baseball league in the country due to prejudice. Some of the best baseball players in the world were unable to play in the major leagues. Monte Irvin was one of them.

Monte Irvin was one of the Negro league's many talented stars. Irvin played for the famous Newark Eagles, who excelled on defense. He had a strong and accurate throwing arm. At the plate, he could hit for power and a high average. There wasn't much Monte Irvin couldn't do on a baseball diamond . . . except gain entrance to baseball's major leagues. Monte Irvin made his debut in the major leagues as a rookie for the New York Giants when he was thirty years old.

Montford "Monte" Irvin was born in Columbia, Alabama, but grew up in Orange, New Jersey. He had an outstanding athletic career at East Orange High School in the 1930s. Irvin earned sixteen letters in a variety of sports. Monte was All-State in football, baseball, and basketball. He also won state titles in track and field.

Irvin later played semipro baseball for a team known as the Orange (New Jersey) Triangles. He enrolled at Lincoln University in Pennsylvania and began to play pro baseball on weekends for the Newark Eagles under the assumed name of Jimmy Nelson. In those days, many athletes, both black and white, played for pay under phony names to protect their amateur status.

Eventually, super baseball star Jimmy Nelson revealed his true secret identity, and Monte Irvin took over his spot in the lineup. Irvin played in five Negro league All-Star games. In 1940, Monte Irvin posted a phenomenal .422 batting average while playing for the Eagles. The following year, his batting average dipped slightly to a stunning .396 average. Monte Irvin then switched to the Mexican league for a season where his hot bat sizzled against south-of-the-border pitching. In sixty-eight games, he clouted thirty home runs and chalked up a .398 batting average. He was named the league's Most Valuable Player.

Monte's sports career was interrupted by World War II, and Irvin served in the U.S. Army until 1945. He then rejoined the Newark Eagles. The Eagles were owned by Effa Manley, who years later became the first woman to be inducted into the Baseball Hall of Fame. Irvin led the Eagles to a pennant and a Negro league World Title in 1946. Monte hit .389 in the regular season and posted a .462 batting average in the championship series. In 1945, Branch Rickey of the Brooklyn Dodgers considered signing Monte Irvin to a contract. The expectation was that Irvin would eventually become the first black athlete to play Major League Baseball. However, Monte Irvin was hesitant about striking a deal with the Dodgers, and negotiations ceased. Jackie Robinson was later signed by Branch Rickey and became the man who broke baseball's color barrier.

Monte Irvin went on to play baseball in Cuba's winter league in 1948–49, where he earned MVP honors. In the summer of 1949, Irvin was signed to a contract by the New York Giants. Monte Irvin finally made it to the major leagues as a thirty-year-old rookie. In 1949, he spent time with the Giants' Jersey City club in the International League and had a .373 batting average. He was called up to the parent club where he joined Giant greats Johnny Mize and Bobby Thomson. Irvin played thirty games for the Giants and had seventeen hits in seventy-six at bats, for a .224 batting average. In 1950, he returned to Jersey City, where he hit .510 and blasted ten home runs in just eighteen games. Monte was mustered out of the International League and assigned to new duty in the Giants' outfield. Irvin played in 112 major-league games in 1950 and had a .299 batting average. He collected 112 hits, which included 19 doubles, 5 triples, and 15 home runs. Monte also amassed sixty-six RBIs.

In 1951, Hank Thompson, Monte Irvin, and Willie Mays combined in the Giants' outfield to form the major league's first all-African American outfield trio. That same season, the New York Giants and the Brooklyn Dodgers engaged in one of the hottest pennant races in baseball history. Monte Irvin contributed to New York's successful run by banging out 174 hits, which added up to a .312 batting average. He also blasted 24 round trippers and chalked up 121 runs batted in, to lead the league in RBIs.

At season's end, the Giants and Dodgers were knotted at the top of the standings and had to play a three-game play-off for the NL pennant and the chance to meet the New York Yankees in the World Series. The Dodgers and Giants split the first two games. The third and deciding game of the play-off took place on October 4, 1951, at New York's Polo Grounds Stadium. In the contest, the Giants were down four to one to the Dodgers, who were led by Duke Snider, Carl

Furillo, and pitcher Don Newcombe. The Giants' hopes for victory faded fast, as the game came down to the last half of the final inning. In the bottom of the ninth, the Giants' Alvin Dark scored on a double by Whitey Lockman with one out, to make the score Giants two and Dodgers four. At that point, Dodgers' hurler Don Newcombe, who had pitched brilliantly, was replaced by Ralph Branca.

New York's Bobby Thomson stepped up to the plate with runners on second and third and one out. What happened is now famously known as "the shot heard round the world." Thomson, who already had two hits in the contest, cranked a Branca fast ball into the left-field stands. The historic home run gave the Giants an amazing 5–4 comeback victory over the Brooklyn Dodgers. The New York Giants captured the pennant on Bobby Thomson's clutch, fence-clearing clout, and earned the right to face the Yankees in the World Series.

Monte Irvin had a fabulous World Series in 1951. Irvin had eleven hits in twenty-four at bats for a fantastic .458 batting average. He also stole home in one game. However, the Yankees, led by Gil McDougald, Hank Bauer, Yogi Berra, Joe DiMaggio, and a young Mickey Mantle, won the World Series crown in six games.

In 1952, Monte Irvin suffered a broken ankle and missed most of the season. He hit .310 but only played in forty-six games. Irvin rebounded in 1953 with a .329 batting average, twenty-one home runs, and ninety-seven runs batted in. Irvin's nineteen home runs and ninety-seven RBIs in 1954 helped the Giants capture the NL pennant and earn a World Series victory over the Cleveland Indians. A member of the Indians club was Larry Doby, another former New Jersey athlete.

In 1955, injuries began to nag at Irvin, and Monte's sweet swing began to slow at the plate. He collected thirty-eight hits in 150 at bats for a .253 average. He was traded to the Chicago Cubs and hit .271 in 1956. Monte had ninety-two hits, which included fifteen home runs. He also added fifty RBIs to his stats. It was his final big-league season.

Over the course of his short, but glorious major-league career, Monte Irvin hit 99 home runs and collected 443 runs batted in. He blasted 731 hits, which included 97 doubles and 31 triples. Irvin posted a .293 career batting average and scored 366 runs.

After retiring as a player, Monte Irvin worked as a scout for the New York Mets and served as a public relations specialist for Baseball Commissioner Bowie Kuhn. Monte Irvin was inducted into the Baseball Hall of Fame in 1973.

DEREK SANDERSON JETER
Baseball
Pequannock, New Jersey
Born: June 26, 1974

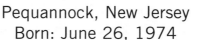

He is the epitome of what New York Yankees baseball stands for. He is cut in the mold of former Yankee greats like Lou Gehrig, Joe DiMaggio, and Don Mattingly. Shortstop Derek Jeter is admired by fans, teammates, and opposing players alike because he plays the game hard, and he plays it clean. Jeter respects the game of baseball. He is a class act on the diamond and off of it. Derek Jeter exudes dignity, determination, and self-discipline. It is almost as if Derek Jeter was born to be a New York Yankee captain.

Derek Jeter was born in Pequannock, New Jersey. His father, Dr. Sanderson Charles Jeter, is African American. His mother, Dorothy, is of German and Irish descent. The Jeter family resided in New Jersey until young Derek was four years old. The Jeters then departed the Garden State for Kalamazoo, Michigan, where young Derek grew up as a fan of the University of Michigan.

Derek Jeter excelled as a basketball and baseball player at Kalamazoo Central High School in Michigan. He earned glowing All-State mentions in basketball and sparkled on the baseball diamond. Jeter hit a sizzling .557 as a high school sophomore. Derek's average slipped to a superb .508 his junior year. He crushed seven home runs and collected twenty-three runs batted in. In fifty-nine at bats, Derek struck out only one time.

Derek Jeter was named the Gatorade High School Player of the Year in 1992. He was also named the American Baseball Coaches Association Player of the Year and the USA Today High School Player of the Year.

Derek, who was an exceptional student, was offered a baseball scholarship to the University of Michigan. Jeter was also the sixth player picked in pro baseball's 1992 amateur draft. He was selected by the New York Yankees. Derek Jeter chose to be a professional baseball player, and a wise choice it was. The sleek-fielding, hard-hitting shortstop spent several seasons tearing up the minor leagues. In 1993, Jeter was voted the Most Outstanding Major League Prospect in the South Atlantic League. In 1994, several newspapers and periodicals, including *Baseball America* and the *Sporting News* named Derek Jeter the Minor League Player of the Year.

Derek Jeter made his major-league debut as a New York Yankee on May 29, 1995, in a game against the Seattle Mariners. Jeter began his prodigious plate assault on opposing big-league pitchers on May 30, 1995, by smacking a single off Seattle hurler Tim Belcher.

In 1995, Jeter played in just fifteen major-league games before returning to the minor leagues. He collected twelve hits in forty-eight at bats in the big time for a .250 bating average.

The young Yankees' infielder became a permanent pinstriper the following year. In 1996, Jeter became the first Yankees' rookie to start at shortstop on opening day since Tom Tresh did it way back in 1962.

Derek quickly became a shortstop sensation and a fan favorite. Jeter led the Yankees with 183 hits and a .312 batting average. He drove in seventy-eight runs and blasted twenty-five doubles, six triples, and ten homers. Jeter also scored 104 runs.

In the 1996 American League Championship Series against the Baltimore Orioles, Derek Jeter was involved in one of baseball's most unusual incidents. The Yanks were losing 4–3 to the Orioles in the bottom of the eighth inning at Yankee Stadium. Jeter was at the plate and launched a deep, high fly ball toward the fence in right field. Baltimore's Tony Tarasco camped under the fly as if to make the catch.

In the stands, twelve-year-old fan Jeffrey Maier of New Jersey leaned over the wall and reached out with the glove he'd brought to the stadium. He snatched Jeter's hit and pulled it into the stands. Baltimore players argued that the ball would have been caught for an out if not for Maier's intervention. The umpires ruled otherwise. Derek Jeter was awarded a home run, which tied the score. The Yankees went on to beat the Orioles in eleven innings on a home run hit by Bernie Williams.

The New York Yankees captured the American League pennant in 1996 and bested the Atlanta Braves four games to two games in the World Series.

Shortstop Derek Jeter was rewarded for his terrific output as a first-year player by being voted the American League's Rookie of the Year. The choice was no surprise to baseball insiders.

"It would have been a surprise if he didn't win it," said Joe Torre, who was then the manager of the Yankees.

Derek followed up his fabulous rookie season by smacking 190 hits in his second year in the major leagues. He batted .291 and scored 106 runs. In 1998, the super shortstop smashed 203 hits, including 19 home runs. He upped his batting average to .324 and his RBI total to eighty-four. The Yankees as a team claimed the World Series crown by sweeping the San Diego Padres four games to none.

Once again Derek Jeter again rocked opposing pitchers in 1999. The Yankees shortstop topped all of his teammates with 219 hits and a bulky .349 batting average. He also clubbed twenty-four home runs, nine triples, and thirty-seven doubles. Derek amassed 102 runs batted in and accounted for 134 runs scored. In the American League, his batting average was second only to Larry Walker of the California Angels, who posted a .379 mark that season.

That same year, the Yankees repeated as World Series winners by besting the Atlanta Braves in four straight games.

The 2000, the New York Yankees continued their winning ways, and so did their shortstop Derek Jeter. Jeter was named to the AL All-Star squad for the third time and became the first New York Yankee in baseball history to be voted the Most Valuable Player of the All-Star game.

Derek collected 201 hits and posted a .339 batting average in helping the Yankees reach the World Series in 2000. The World Championship was a subway series against the NL champions, the New York Mets. Jeter ripped up the pitching staff of his crosstown rivals to capture the World Series' Most Valuable Player Award. The Yanks easily topped the Mets in five contests to retain baseball's coveted crown for a third straight year.

Derek Jeter hit a solid .311 in 2001 with twenty-one home runs and seventy-four runs batted in. However, the sure-handed shortstop's high point of the season was a slick play on a relay throw in the AL Division Series against the Oakland A's.

The Yankees had lost the first two games of their series against the A's. They were leading 1–0 in the seventh inning of game three, when their lead seemed ready to evaporate. Oakland's Jeremy Giambi attempted to score on another player's double to right. Yankee right fielder Shane Spencer's throw home was off-line and missed the cutoff man. Derek Jeter raced across the infield, snared the errant throw, and made a fantastic flip of the ball to catcher Jorge Posada at the plate. Giambi was tagged out on a play deemed one of baseball's most amazing defensive maneuvers. The Yankees coasted to a 1–0 victory after the phenomenal flip, and eventually ousted the Orioles. New York captured the American League pennant but lost to the Arizona Diamondbacks in the World Series, four games to three.

Yankee shortstop Derek Jeter became the first major leaguer to hit a home run in the month of November during the 2001 World Series.

In 2002, Jeter hit .297 with seventy-five runs batted in. He crossed the plate a total of 124 times that season.

Infielder Derek Jeter was named the captain of the New York Yankees in 2003. Derek's batting average rebounded to .324 that year, and New York captured the American League pennant. However, the Yankees were stymied in their quest for baseball's ultimate crown in the World Series by the Florida Marlins.

The "Prince of Pinstripes" collected 188 hits in 2004. Jeter cracked twenty-three round trippers and stroked a career-high forty-four doubles. His doubles mark set a single-season record.

"He's the heart of this team," said superstar teammate Alex Rodriguez about Derek Jeer in 2004. Jeter won his first American League Gold Glove Award in 2004. On August 24, 2004, Derek Jeer scored the one thousandth run of his baseball career in a 5–4 Yankee victory over the Cleveland Indians.

In 2005, Jeter hit .309 and slugged nineteen home runs. He crashed his very first major-league grand slam on June 18, 2005, in an interleague contest against the Chicago Cubs. The Yankees won that game 8–1.

The Yankee captain posted excellent numbers at the plate in 2006. Derek Jeter blasted fourteen home runs and recorded a .344 batting average. On May 26, 2006, Derek collected his two thousandth career hit in a game against the Kansas City Royals. In the 2006 American League Division Series against the Detroit Tigers, the Yankee shortstop got five hits in five at bats, leading his team to an 8–1 victory.

Derek Jeter has become the face of the Yankees over his baseball career. He is as recognizable as pinstripe icons Babe Ruth, Phil Rizzuto, and Mickey Mantle. Jeter is considered the most marketable player in baseball. He is handsome, articulate, intelligent, and poised under pressure. Most of all, Derek Jeter, the clean-cut captain of the New York Yankees, is a man of respect . . . and he's earned it!

Derek Jeter–Courtesy New York Yankees

In 2008 Derek Jeter collected the 2,416th hit of his career to pass Mickey Mantle on the N.Y. Yankees All-Time Hit List

Derek Jeter–Courtesy New York Yankees

ALOIS TERRY "AL" LEITER
Baseball
Toms River, New Jersey
Born: October 23, 1965

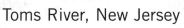

The professional sports journey of this articulate pitching ace began at Central Regional High School in Bayville, New Jersey. Lean, mound-mean, lefty Al Leiter traveled from his birthplace in Toms River, New Jersey, across the Hudson to the fabled home of the world-famous Bronx Bombers. Al Leiter began his major-league career with the New York Yankees and concluded his baseball career in pinstripes. Along the way, in his roundabout march to diamond notoriety, Leiter collected world championship rings in frosty Toronto, Canada, and in the sunshine state of Florida. For a time, he also settled into the starting rotation of the Yankees' crosstown hardball rivals, the New York Mets.

Al Leiter signed with the Yankees and began his professional mound career in 1984. He spent several years pitching his way through the minors and compiled a less-than-impressive record of fifteen wins and twenty-five losses. However, Leiter struck out a total of 321 batters, and for the most part posted decent earned run averages. In 1987, the Yankees summoned Al Leiter to the show, and he appeared in four games, winning two and losing two.

The six foot three inch, 220-pound southpaw appeared in fourteen games for the Yankees in 1988 and posted a 4–4 record with a 3.92 earned run average. He also whiffed sixty big-league batters.

From 1988 to 1992, Big Al seesawed between the major and minor leagues. In 1988, he spent time with the Yankees before being traded to the Toronto Blue Jays for outfielder Jesse Barfield. A series of shoulder injuries hindered his progress, and he ended up having arthroscopic surgery on the shoulder of his pitching arm. However, Leiter was a member of the 1992 Blue Jays' club that captured the 1993 World Series crown by beating the Atlanta Braves four games to two games.

In 1993, Al Leiter returned to the pitching mound healthy and hungry. He appeared in thirty-four games for the Blue Jays and chalked up nine wins against only six losses. Leiter appeared in five postseason contests, helping Toronto once again reach the world series. The Blue Jays were matched against the potent Philadelphia Phillies. Leiter picked up a World Series win in relief in game one, and even managed to bang out a double when he stepped up to the plate. Toronto went on to top Philadelphia four games to two games in the World Series. The

Blue Jays squad, including a southpaw hurler named Al Leiter, were once again crowned World Champions.

Leiter remained in Toronto for two more seasons, posting records of 6–7 in 1994 and 11–11 in 1995. He was then signed by the Florida Marlins as a free agent and jumped from the American League to the National League.

Al's move to the Marlins proved to be an intelligent maneuver. Leiter posted big numbers and earned a berth on the National League All-Star squad. The lanky lefty was 16–12 on the mound, with a 2.93 earned run average. Leiter also recorded two hundred strikeouts.

On May 11, 1996, Al pitched a no-hitter against the Colorado Rockies. The Marlins recorded an 11–0 shutout victory in that contest. It was the first no-hitter in the history of the Florida Marlins franchise.

The following year, Leiter went 11–9 on the hill and helped the Marlins advance to the World Series. Florida's opponent in the championship was the Cleveland Indians. The series proved to be an exciting nip-and-tuck battle between two talented ball clubs. The championship came down to the final game of the series. Each club had three victories when they met in a seventh game, which would determine who wore baseball's coveted World Championship crown. Al Leiter took the mound for the Marlins in that key contest. Leiter did not disappoint. He pitched six strong innings, giving up two runs on four hits. Al left the game with no decision, but positioned his club for victory down the stretch. The Blue Jays bested the Indians three to two in extra innings to win the 1997 World Series.

"It was the most exciting, pressure-packed game of my baseball career," Leiter said later.

During the off-season Al Leiter was traded to the New York Mets. He returned home to the East Coast to join a Mets team that included catcher Mike Piazza, infielder Robin Ventura, and pitcher John Franco. Al Leiter fit in well with his new teammates, and enjoyed a banner season, posting a career-high seventeen wins (17–6) and a career low era of 2.47.

In 1999, Leiter won thirteen games and lost twelve games. On August 1,1999, Al struck out a career-high fifteen batters in the Mets' 5–4 victory over the Chicago Cubs. At the end of the season, the New York Mets ended up tied with the Cincinnati Reds for the National League's wild-card berth in the play-offs. The Mets and the Reds were forced into a one-game play-off to determine which team would go to the National League play-offs.

Once again, Al Leiter got the ball in a key, winner-take-all situation and responded admirably. Leiter pitched a complete-game, 5–0 shutout to send the Mets into the play-offs. Eventually, the Mets lost to the Atlanta Braves in the National League Championship Series.

The year 2000 was an all-star season for the Mets' Al Leiter. He won sixteen games and lost eight. Leiter was voted to the All-Star squad for the second time in his career. In July of 2000, a victory over the Atlanta Braves earned Al Leiter the two hundredth victory of his pitching career.

The New York Mets battled their way into the World Series in 2000 by besting the Saint Louis Cardinals in the National League Championship. The American League champions who opposed the Mets in the 2000 World Series were none other than the New York Yankees.

Al Leiter started game one and game five of the classic New York subway series and pitched well. He recorded sixteen strikeouts and kept his earned run average well under three in 15 2/3 innings pitched. Nevertheless, the Mets dropped both contests and went on to be bested by the powerful Bronx Bombers, four games to one game.

Al Leiter remained a Met until the end of the 2004 season. On April 30, 2002, Leiter defeated the Arizona Diamondbacks, to add an historic feat to his noteworthy pitching resume. The win made Al Leiter the first pitcher to defeat all thirty major-league teams. In his seven seasons as a New York Met, Al Leiter won ninety-five games and lost sixty-seven contests.

In 2004, Leiter became a free agent and was claimed by the Florida Marlins. Leiter's second stint with "the Fish" was far less productive than his earlier days in Florida. In July of 2005, Al was acquired by the New York Yankees. He returned to the place where his big-league career had begun. After years as a starting pitcher, Al Leiter informed Yankees' manager Joe Torre he'd be willing to work out of the bull pen. Al Leiter closed out his career doing relief work in pinstripes. The last game he pitched in was on October 2, 2005, at Yankee Stadium. Al started his big-league career as a Yankee, and he finished his major-league career as a Yankee with a mound victory.

Al Leiter now works as a television analyst for New York Yankees broadcasts and is active in numerous charitable organizations.

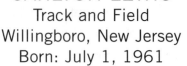

CARLTON LEWIS
Track and Field
Willingboro, New Jersey
Born: July 1, 1961

Winning a gold medal at the Olympic Games is an astonishing exhibition of superb athleticism. Winning more than one gold medal immortalizes an athlete's accomplishments. New Jersey's Carl Lewis won a mind-boggling total of nine Olympic gold medals over the course of his spectacular sports career.

Carlton Lewis was born in Birmingham, Alabama, but grew up in Willingboro, New Jersey. Carl was the third son of two track coaches. The Lewis Family was very athletic, and for a time Carl seemed to be the least gifted of the group when it came to sports. He was always small for his age. Suddenly at the age of fifteen, Carl sprouted into a magnificent physical specimen. At age sixteen Carl Lewis ran the 100-meter dash in 10.6 seconds. Carl also long jumped twenty-three feet, nine inches. People no longer doubted Carl's ability as an athlete.

In 1979, Carl Lewis graduated from high school in New Jersey and entered the University of Houston. He quickly established himself as a top competitor on a national level in track and field. Lewis captured the NCAA Long Jump Championship in 1980. The following year, Carl was the NCAA and National Outdoor champion in both the long jump and the 100-meter dash. In 1981, he was ranked number one in the world in those two events.

Carl Lewis decided to leave school in 1981 to join the Santa Monica Track Club. Lewis wanted to focus on his athletic training without having any distractions. Carl Lewis once again won national championships in the long jump and 100-meter dash in 1982. The next year, Lewis won the 100-meter dash and the 200-meter dash at the U.S. Nationals. He added a third U.S. National title by taking first place in the long jump in 1983.

Track-and-field fans began to refer to the six foot two inch, 175-pound superman as "King Carl." Lewis was the invincible ruler when it came to the 100-meter dash and the long jump. Carl easily made the 1984 U.S. Olympic squad.

The 1984 Olympics were held in Los Angeles, California. Carl Lewis stole the show by capturing four gold medals. Lewis won the 200-meter dash in a time of 19.80. Carl soared to victory in the long jump with a leap of 28 feet 1/4 inch. He took home a gold medal in the 4 x 100 relay by pairing up with Sam Graddy, Ron Brown, and Calvin Smith. Most impressive of all was Carl Lewis's lightning-fast performance in the 100-meter dash. Lewis ran the one hundred meters in 9.99 seconds. He was clocked at running twenty-eight miles per hour at the finish. Winning the event made America's Carl Lewis the fastest man in the world!

On May 5, 1987, Carl Lewis's father passed away. At the funeral, Carl took the gold medal he'd won in the 100-meter at the 1984 Olympic Games and placed it beside his father. "I want you to have this because it was your favorite event," he whispered. Carl's mother, who was standing with her son, seemed a bit shocked by Carl's parting gift to his dad. "Don't worry," Carl said to his mother, "I'll get another one."

Carl made good on his promise at the 1988 Olympic Games in Seoul, South Korea. Lewis streaked to a gold-medal victory in the 100-meter dash with a sizzling time of 9.92 seconds. (Canada's Ben Johnson actually beat Lewis in the race, but was later disqualified when he tested positive for steroids.) Lewis was awarded the gold for running a clean race at a blazing pace. Carl finished second in the 200-meter dash, but his 4 x 10 meter relay team was disqualified on a failed baton pass from Calvin Smith to Lee McNeill. However, Carl Lewis once again struck gold in the long jump with an impressive leap of 28 feet 7 1/4 inches. Carl Lewis's medal total in two Olympiads was six gold medals and one silver.

Carl Lewis, who was always an outspoken advocate of clean and fair competition, boycotted the 1989 National Championships. Lewis felt the Athletic Congress was not doing enough to stop drug use by track-and-field athletes. In 1991, Carl Lewis returned to competition and ran in the World Championships. He sped to a first-place finish in the 100-meter dash. King Carl made a third appearance at the Olympic Games in 1992. That year, the games were held in Barcelona, Spain. Lewis repeated as a gold medalist in the long jump, rocketing 28 feet 5 1/4 inches through the air before touching down to earth. He also earned gold running in the 4 x 100 meter relay. The King's royal vault now held a total of eight gold medals.

Mel Rose, the coach of the U.S. team, was totally amazed by Carl Lewis's athletic prowess. "Carl is the greatest athlete I've have ever seen," said Rose.

Finally in 1996, Carl Lewis returned to mine Olympic gold one final time. At the Olympic Games in Atlanta, Georgia, Carl Lewis gracefully soared through the southern sky to victory. He leaped 27 feet 10 3/4 inches to finish first in the long jump. Carl Lewis won his ninth Olympic gold medal. It was a fitting finish to King Carl's masterful reign at the Olympic Games.

Carl Lewis's amazing accomplishments did not go unnoticed or unrewarded. In 1981, Lewis won the Sullivan Award as America's outstanding amateur athlete. Carl was named the Associated Press Male Athlete of the Year. Carl Lewis repeated as the AP Male Athlete of the Year in 1983. In 1985, New Jersey's Carl Lewis was inducted into the Olympic Hall of Fame. King Carl Lewis was named to the National Track and Field Hall of Fame in 2001.

VINCENT T. LOMBARDI
Football
Englewood, New Jersey
Born: June 11, 1913

Football coach Vince Lombardi once said, "The difference between a successful person and others is not a lack of strength, not a lack of knowledge, but rather a lack of will."

Vincent Thomas Lombardi was a man who often imposed his will upon others, especially while playing or coaching football. Lombardi's iron will, fierce determination, and no-nonsense attitude made him extremely successful in athletics and also in life.

Vince Lombardi was born in Brooklyn, New York, but had deep roots in the Garden State of New Jersey. Lombardi attended public school in the Sheepshead Bay area of Brooklyn. After elementary school, Vince, who was a devout Catholic, entered Cathedral Prep to study for the priesthood. After four years at Cathedral Prep, Vince Lombardi came to the realization that he was best suited for a different vocation. Vince transferred to St. Francis Prep and devoted his energy to the sport of football. Lombardi proved to be a holy terror on the gridiron and won a football scholarship to Fordham University in New York. Vince Lombardi and Alex Wojciechowicz, along with their offensive line mates meshed into a formidable front wall, which won national fame as "Fordham's Seven Blocks of Granite."

Vince Lombardi graduated from Fordham in 1937. He worked for a finance company and attended law school at night. Once again, Lombardi deduced that his life's path lay in a different direction. It was back to the gridiron for Vince Lombardi. Vince accepted a position as an assistant football coach at St. Cecilia's High School in Englewood, New Jersey. The head coach at St. Cecelia's was Andy Palu, a former college teammate of Lombardi's at Fordham. Andy Palu had been a quarterback for the Fordham Ram's gridiron squad. In 1942, Andy Palu left St. Cecelia's to take a job at Fordham University. Vince Lombardi became the head football coach at St. Cecelia's High School.

Lombardi remained the gridiron mentor at St. Cecelia's in New Jersey for the next five years. In all, Vince Lombardi spent eight years as a New Jersey high school football coach. In 1947, Coach Lombardi returned to Fordham and stayed with the Fordham Rams until 1948. He then joined the coaching corps of football immortal Colonel Red Blaik at the United States Military Academy at West Point. Lombardi sharpened his coaching skills at West Point until 1953.

In 1954, iron-willed Vince Lombardi was ready to test his coaching methods in the National Football League. Lombardi began his career as a pro-football coach with the New York Giants under head coach Jim Lee Howell. Vince Lombardi was forty-one years old at the time. Another assistant coach on that Giants' squad during that period was Tom Landry. Landry went on to have a brilliant head-coaching career with the Dallas Cowboys.

Head coach Jim Lee Howell, with a little help from his assistants Vince Lombardi and Tom Landry, guided the New York Giants to the NFL Championship in 1956.

Vince Lombardi finally got a chance to call his own shots as an NFL head coach in 1959, when he was hired by the Green Bay Packers. The Packers were a lowly NFL cellar-dweller squad at the time. They had lost ten of twelve gridiron contests the season before. Lombardi resolved to quickly rectify that downward spiral.

"The price of success is hard work, dedication to the job at hand, and the determination that whether we win or lose we have applied the best of ourselves to the task at hand," Lombardi professed. Lombardi's manifesto became Green Bay gridiron gospel. He prodded and pushed his players to their physical limits in practice. Lombardi's rugged and relentless work ethic paid instant dividends. The Packers won seven games in 1959 and lost only five contests. In 1960, the Packers made it to the NFL Championship game, but lost to the Philadelphia Eagles by a 13–17 score. After that bitter postseason defeat, Coach Vince Lombardi went on to earn victories in his next nine postseason games. In 1961 and 1962, the Packers, with Lombardi at the helm, won NFL Championships. Green Bay earned another NFL crown in 1965.

The year 1966 was an historic one for pro football. The National Football League and the American Football League agreed to meet in a postseason championship contest dubbed "the Super Bowl." The NFL Champion Green Bay Packers, coached by Vince Lombardi, took on the AFL Champion Kansas City Chiefs, coached by Hank Stram, in Super Bowl I on January 15, 1967, in Los Angeles's Memorial Coliseum. The Packers posted a decisive 35–10 victory.

Green Bay repeated as the NFL Champion the next season and made an encore appearance in the Super Bowl. This time, the Packers' opponents were the AFL Champion Oakland Raiders, coached by John Rauch. The game was played January 14, 1968, at Miami's Orange Bowl Stadium. Once again, Lombardi's squad thumped Oakland by a 33–14 score. Vince Lombardi captured his second Super Bowl title.

Vince Lombardi stepped down as the Packers' head coach after his second consecutive Super Bowl triumph. He served as Green Bay's general manager in 1968. The Washington Redskins hired Lombardi as their head coach in 1969. The Redskins posted a record of seven wins, five losses, and two ties that season.

Vince Lombardi was diagnosed with intestinal cancer in 1970. He died September 3, 1970, at age fifty-seven.

Vince Lombardi was an iron-willed coach, who truly believed that hard work, determination, and dedication resulted in success in sports and in life. As a professional football coach, Lombardi posted a total career record of 105 wins, 35 losses, and 6 ties. His teams won five NFL Championships and two Super Bowls. The trophy awarded to the victors of pro football's Super Bowl is named in honor of Coach Vincent T. Lombardi. Vince Lombardi is also a member of the Pro Football Hall of Fame.

Vince Lombardi–Courtesy Fordham University Sports Information

Offensive linemen Vince Lombardi and Alex Wojciechowski were two of Fordham University's Famous Seven Blocks of Granite

Vince Lombardi–Courtesy Fordham University Sports Information

ED MARINARO
Football
New Milford, New Jersey
Born: March 31, 1950

He was the Ivy League phenom who shocked big-time college gridiron fans by leading the nation in scoring, rushing, and all-purpose yards.

Ed Marinaro was born in New York, New York, but later migrated to New Milford, New Jersey, with his family. Marinaro was an excellent student and a star athlete at New Milford High School. After graduation, he enrolled at Cornell University. The rigid demands of an Ivy League education did not prevent Marinaro from establishing himself as a class act on the collegiate gridiron. He became a starting running back for the Big Red during his second year at Cornell and was almost instantly touted as a sophomore sensation. Marinaro was big, strong, and shifty. He was tough to tackle. Ed could run over defenders or streak past them. He was just fast enough to leave would-be tacklers in his dust.

Ed Marinaro's banner seasons at Cornell were in 1970 and 1971. In 1970, junior Ed Marinaro topped all college runners in the country by rumbling for 1,425 yards on 285 carries. Ed gained an average of 158.3 yards per game that season. The following year, Marinaro methodically marched his way into the gridiron record books.

In 1971, Ed Marinaro led the nation in scoring with 148 points on 24 touchdowns and 4 extra points. He averaged 16.4 points per game. That same season, he repeated as America's best running back. He gained 1,881 yards on 356 carries to lead the nation. Amazingly, Ed averaged 209.0 yards per gridiron contest. Ed Marinaro also led the nation in all-purpose yards in 1971. He totaled 1,932 all-purpose yards for an average of 214.7 all-purpose yards per game.

Cornell's Ed Marinaro was a tireless, one-man offensive machine. His output was nothing less than astonishing.

Marinaro was the first running back in NCAA history to gain over four thousand rushing yards. Marinaro's total of 4,715 rushing yards stood as the high-water mark for college books for many years. Ed's career rushing average of 174.6 yards per game is still at the top of the list in that category.

In 1971, Ed Marinaro was named a First Team All-American. He won the Maxwell Trophy as the outstanding college football player in the nation and finished second to Auburn quarterback Pat Sullivan in the Heisman Trophy balloting.

Ed Marinaro was picked by the Minnesota Vikings in the second round of the 1972 NFL draft. He was the fiftieth player selected. Marinaro played with the Vikings until 1975. Ed then spent a year as a back for the New York Jets (1976) and a year with the Seattle Seahawks (1977) before retiring from pro football. In the NFL, Ed Marinaro never achieved the stardom he had experienced in the college ranks. However, Marinaro did go on to a degree of stardom in a field other than athletics.

Ed Marinaro enjoyed a long career as an actor in movies and television. Marinaro appeared as a regular cast member on *The Edge of Night* serial, the hit comedy show *Laverne and Shirley*, the police drama *Hill Street Blues*, and many other shows.

Ed Marinaro is also a member of the College Football Hall of Fame.

Ed Marinaro–Courtesy Minnesota Vikings Football

JOSEPH MICHAEL MEDWICK
Baseball
Carteret, New Jersey
Born: November 24, 1911

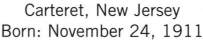

They dubbed him "Ducky" because he seemed to waddle a bit when he walked. Joe Medwick didn't much care for the waterfowl moniker laid on him by fans and teammates. Medwick preferred his other nickname, which was "Muscles." Few dared call Joe "Ducky" to his face, because the name ruffled the feathers of the hot-tempered Muscles Medwick. Joe got back at those who callously called him Ducky the best way he knew how. He vented his wrath on the pitches of opposing hurlers. Joe "Ducky" Medwick beat up on any ball a pitcher dared to throw over the fat part of the plate. Medwick was one of baseball's great all-time hitters.

Joe Medwick was born in Carteret, New Jersey. He was the son of Hungarian immigrant parents, and he grew up dreaming of playing college football for the Fightin' Irish of Notre Dame. The five foot ten inch, 187-pound Medwick was a great, all-around athlete who especially excelled in baseball. In the 1930s, he began to play baseball for pay. To protect his amateur status and his gridiron hopes of someday playing for Notre Dame, Medwick used the name "Mickey King." After young Mickey King hit .419 in baseball's minor leagues, Joe Medwick had an epiphany. Baseball was his true calling! Mickey King's name vanished from baseball lineups, and Joe Medwick's name magically appeared in its place.

In 1932, Joe "Ducky" Medwick joined a rough-and-tumble group of baseball rascals eventually known as the Gas House Gang. In major-league baseball circles, they were better known as the Saint Louis Cardinals. The group included Frankie Frisch, Pepper Martin, Jim Bottomley, and Dizzy Dean. Medwick played in twenty-six major-league games his first year in the bigs, and collected thirty-seven hits in 106 at bats for a .349 average.

In 1933, Cardinals' second baseman Frankie Frisch became Saint Louis's player-manager, and Joe Medwick became a mainstay in the outfield for the Gas House Gang. Medwick belted 182 hits and posted a .306 batting average. He had forty doubles, ten triples, and eighteen home runs.

Medwick hit .319 in 1934 and helped the Saint Louis Cardinals capture the National League pennant. In the 1934 World Series against the Detroit Tigers, Ducky Medwick was involved in one of the strangest episodes in major-league history. The series was tied three games apiece when the clubs faced off in Detroit for the seventh and deciding game of the series. Medwick was personally having a phenomenal series. In the seventh inning, he smacked a triple to drive home two runs, which made the score 9–0 in favor of the Cardinals. It was Ducky's eleventh hit of the series. As he slid into third just ahead of the relay throw, Detroit third baseman Marvin Owen jumped to catch the ball. When he came down, he almost spiked Medwick who was sprawled in the dirt. The quick-tempered Hungarian Hercules took offense to the play and kicked his cleats up at Owens. The crowd howled at what they thought was a dirty play by Medwick. It was really just a bang-bang baseball reaction.

After the inning ended and Joe Medwick went to play right field, the home-town crowd continued to jeer at him. When Ducky reached the outfield, the Detroit fans in the stands began to toss things at the Cardinals' outfielder. They threw fruit, vegetables, rolled-up pieces of paper, bottles, and anything else they could lay their hands on. The gale of garbage continued until right field was filled with more rubbish than a trash heap. The game was halted, but the downpour of debris continued.

Finally, Kenesaw Mountain Landis, the commissioner of baseball, who was seated in a private box near the first-base side of the stadium, summoned the Cardinals' outfielder to his box. Landis questioned the Cardinals' outfielder about the play in an attempt to calm the irate fans.

"It was just one of those things that happen in a ball game," Medwick said, shrugging off the incident.

Saint Louis Cardinals' manager Frankie Frisch made this comment about the typhoon of fan trash: "They wouldn't do that if Joe had a bat in his hands," said Frisch. "He'd kill somebody."

The bombardment continued, much to the distress of the baseball commissioner. He ordered Joe Medwick removed from the game more for his own personal protection than for punishment. The Cardinals went on to win game seven without Ducky in right field and captured the 1934 World Series crown.

Joe "Ducky" Medwick went on a hitting spree over the next few seasons. In 1935, he pounded out 224 hits in 634 at bats for a fat .353 batting average. Among his many hits were forty-six doubles, thirteen triples, and twenty-three home runs.

In 1936, Medwick drove in 138 runners to win the National League's RBI title. He also bashed 223 hits and had a .351 batting average. Just when it seemed that Ducky Medwick couldn't do much better, he did. The year 1937 was the banner season of his splendid career.

Joe Medwick became one of only six National League players to ever win baseball's coveted Triple Crown for his on-field performance in 1937. Medwick won the NL batting crown with a .374 average. He captured the RBI title by driving in 154 runs. Ducky also shared the home run crown with Mel Ott of the New York Giants. Medwick and Ott each crushed thirty-one homers in 1937. To top off his amazing accomplishments that season, Joe "Ducky" Medwick was voted the National League's Most Valuable Player.

Ducky didn't slow down at the plate after his Herculean assault on opposing pitching in 1937. He drove in 122 runs in 1938, to take the National League RBI crown for the third straight season. He belted twenty-one home runs, eight triples, and forty-seven doubles among his 190 hits. Joe's batting average was a solid .322.

In 1939, Medwick's batting average rose to .332. It was the ninth straight year he'd hit .300 or better. He also collected over two hundred hits in a season for the fourth time. Despite his solid stats, Ducky was dealt to the Brooklyn Dodgers in 1940.

The change of scenery didn't affect Medwick's awesome output at the plate. He batted .300 and racked up forty-four extra-base hits, which included fourteen home runs. Ducky teamed with Dodger greats Pee Wee Reese, Cookie Lavagetto, and Mickey Owen to capture the National League pennant in 1941. Brooklyn's terrific outfield trio of Pete Reiser (.343 BA), Dixie Walker (.311 BA), and Joe Medwick (.318 BA) all finished among the top ten hitters in the NL that season. Unfortunately for the Dodgers, they lost the New York subway World Series to a Yankees club led by Joe DiMaggio, Phil Rizzuto, and Bill Dickey.

Medwick spent the next two seasons in Brooklyn, hitting .300 in 1942 and .272 in a half season's work in 1943. Ducky spent the remainder of the 1943 season with the New York Giants and had a .281 batting average. He remained a New York Giant for two more seasons and regained his old form at the plate. Medwick posted a .337 batting average in 1944 and was hitting at a .304 clip in 1945 when he was traded to the Boston Braves. Joe finished out the 1945 season with the Braves and had a .284 average.

Age started to catch up with Ducky, and it slowed down his swing just a bit. As a part-time player with the Brooklyn Dodgers in 1946, he hit .312 in just forty-one games.

Joe "Ducky" Medwick finished his career where it had all started: in Saint Louis with the Cardinals. He appeared in seventy-five games for the Cardinals in

1947 and posted a .307 average. In 1948, Ducky Medwick played in only twenty games and hit well below his usual average.

For a while, Joe Medwick worked as a player-coach in the minor leagues. He then became the Saint Louis Cardinals' minor-league hitting instructor and held that post until 1975.

Joseph "Muscles" Medwick was inducted into the Baseball Hall of Fame in 1968. He died of heart attack at spring training on March 21, 1975, at sixty-three years of age.

SAMUEL D. MILLS
Football
Neptune, New Jersey
Born: June 3, 1959

He was the small, middle linebacker who had a big heart and always made the big plays. Big hitter Sam Mills of Neptune, New Jersey, battled NFL behemoths in the gridiron trenches and more often than not emerged from the football fray victorious. Mills made the tackles! He was fast, fearless, and a ferocious hitter.

Sam Mills stood only five feet nine inches tall, but he was a standout football player and wrestler at Long Branch High School in New Jersey. He attended Montclair State University, where he continued to roam the gridiron from his middle linebacker position. In 1980, senior Sam Mills was named a Kodak All-American. While at Montclair State, Mills established school records for career tackles (501), single-season tackles (142), and single-game tackles (22). Three times over the course of his four-year college career, he was named Defensive Player of the Year by the New Jersey Collegiate Football Writers Association. Sam Mills was a respected team leader and an instinctive football player. Nevertheless, Mills was shunned by pro scouts because of his height. The Cleveland Browns signed Mills to a free-agent contract in 1981 but in truth had little confidence in his ability to play in the National Football League. Mills was a quick cut during the Browns' training camp.

Sam Mills, the ninth of eleven children in his family, was not easily discouraged by rejection. He believed in himself and in his ability to play professional football. Mills decided to try an alternate route to the NFL. In 1982, he signed a contract with the Toronto Argonauts of the Canadian Football League. Years earlier, fellow New Jersey athlete Joe Theismann had quarterbacked for the Argos and used the CFL as a springboard to the NFL. Unfortunately, the Canadian League springboard plan failed. Mills was bounced out of the Argonauts' training camp,

Sam Mills persisted in pursuing a pro-football career. Luck was on his side. In 1983, a new professional league, known as the United States Football League began operation. Sam Mills signed with the Philadelphia Stars team of the USFL, which was coached by Jim Mora. At last, linebacker Sam Mills found his pro-football niche. Mills quickly established himself as one of the league's stellar defensive players. He also became a fan favorite, first in Philadelphia, and then in Baltimore, where the Stars relocated for the 1985 season.

Sam Mills helped his Stars squad capture league titles in 1983 and 1984. Mills was also elected to the USFL All-Star team three consecutive times.

In his three seasons in the United States Football League, Sam Mills made 592 tackles, had 9 pass interceptions, and recovered 10 fumbles. He played every defensive down of every game, which is a testament to his overall strength and durability.

When the USFL went bankrupt, Stars' coach Jim Mora became the head coach of the NFL's New Orleans Saints. Jim Mora went to New Orleans, and Sam Mills moved with his mentor. Sam's lack of height was no longer a concern. Mills had more than proved he could play and play well with the really big boys of the gridiron.

Sam Mills started at middle linebacker for the New Orleans Saints from 1986 to 1994. In Sam's rookie year in the NFL he registered ninety-two tackles. During his nine seasons with the Saints, the athlete the scouts had said was too short to play professional football was voted to the NFL Pro Bowl four times (1987, 1988, 1991, and 1992). In 1994, his final season as a Saints' linebacker, Sam Mills made a career-high 115 tackles.

Sam Mills then signed with the Carolina Panthers and played for the NFL expansion club from 1995 to 1997. Sam started every game during that span, which is an exceptional achievement for a NFL linebacker in his late thirties. In 1966, Sam Mills was named to the Pro Bowl for a fifth time. Mills retired from pro football in 1997, after spending a total of twelve years in the NFL. His career stats were stunning. Mills made a total of 1,319 tackles 20.5 quarterback sacks, and 11 interceptions. He also scored four touchdowns on defense. Sam Mills concluded his pro career as a man respected and admired by coaches, players, and fans.

Tragically, Sam Mills was diagnosed with intestinal cancer in 2003 and passed away on April 18, 2005. He was only forty-five years old when he died, but he left behind a remarkable sports legacy.

Sam Mills's high school and NFL football jerseys are on permanent display in the Long Branch High School gym. The home field of the Montclair State football team is renamed in honor of Sam Mills. The Most Valuable Player trophy awarded annually to Montclair State's top football player is also named after Sam Mills.

The New Orleans Saints and the Carolina Panthers have both retired Sam Mills' number fifty-one Mills has been enshrined in the New Orleans Saints Hall of Fame and the Carolina Panthers Hall of Honor. In addition, Sam Mills was voted into both the Louisiana Sports Hall of Fame and the Sports Hall of Fame of New Jersey. For an athlete who was only five feet nine inches tall, Sam Mills stood tall on the gridiron and in life.

Sam Mills–Courtesy Carolina Panthers Football

SHAUN O'HARA

Football
Hillsborough, New Jersey
Born: June 23, 1977

Shaun O'Hara was a college football walk-on player who defied all odds and followed a gridiron path that eventually led to a Super Bowl championship.

O'Hara was born in Chicago, Illinois, and spent part of his early childhood in Medina, Ohio. He played high school sports in Hillsborough, New Jersey. While at Somerset County High School, Shaun excelled in football, basketball, and track. He was a good athlete, but not a star player. O'Hara was hardworking, dedicated, and intelligent. He was driven to succeed. As a high school freshman who stood six feet one inch tall and weighed 230 pounds, O'Hara told his coaches his goal was to eventually play professional football. It was just a far-fetched dream at the time. However, dreams do come true.

Shaun O'Hara did not receive a full sports scholarship. After he graduated from Hillsborough High School, Shaun enrolled at Rutgers, The State University of New Jersey and was granted permission to try out for the football team as a walk-on. O'Hara's never-say-die work ethic, along with his intelligence and attitude, earned him a spot on the 1995 Scarlet Knights squad as a tight end. After several position switches, Shaun found a home on the offensive line and earned himself a scholarship.

Shaun O'Hara shined as a Scarlet Knight and earned Second Team All-East honors in 1998. In 1999, O'Hara was named captain of a Rutgers football squad that included future NFL stars Gary Brackett and L. J. Smith.

The walk-on who still dreamed of playing in the National Football League earned All Big East First Team honors his senior season. O'Hara was also named the Knights' Outstanding Offensive Lineman for the second year in a row. Additionally, Shaun was awarded Rutgers's prized gridiron trophy, the Paul Robeson Award, which is given to the athlete who had the greatest impact on Rutgers football during his career. Shaun O'Hara ended his college-football career by playing in the Hula Bowl All-Star game.

Shaun O'Hara's collegiate gridiron accomplishments were notable, but not outstanding enough to impress professional scouts. O'Hara was not selected in the NFL draft. Once again, his lifelong dream seemed to be in jeopardy. Shaun was forced to trod the long, hard road taken by free agents if he wanted to play pro football. O'Hara signed a free-agent contract with the Cleveland Browns in April of 2000. Tireless work, gridiron smarts, and unwavering determination helped O'Hara make the Cleveland Browns squad. His dream was finally realized.

In November of 2000, center Shaun O'Hara made his first NFL start. O'Hara spent three seasons as a starter on the offensive line for the Browns. During that time he even managed to catch a two-yard touchdown pass from Cleveland quarterback Tim Couch. In 2004, Shaun left the Browns and signed with the New York Giants. O'Hara became the Giants' starting center and anchored Big Blue's offensive line. In 2005, he was named an alternate to the NFC Pro Bowl squad. In 2006, Shaun O'Hara was named the Giants' Man of the Year for his work on the gridiron and in the community. He was also selected as one of the Giants' captains. Shaun O'Hara found himself living the dream he had as a high school freshman in Hillsborough, New Jersey.

The dream got even better in 2008. Shaun O'Hara and the New York Giants defeated the Green Bay Packers to capture the NFC title and earned a trip to Super Bowl XLII. The Giants were matched against the undefeated New England Patriots in the 2008 Super Bowl. The impossible dream was realized, and the Giants defeated the heavily favored Patriots 17–14 to capture the Super Bowl championship. Shaun O'Hara, the high school athlete who did not win a full football scholarship, the college walk-on, and the undrafted pro free agent, earned himself a Super Bowl ring along with his Giants teammates.

A week after the Giants' amazing Super Bowl triumph, Shaun O'Hara returned to the Rutgers University campus in New Jersey to address fans at a Scarlet Knights' basketball contest. "I'm hoping to finish my career wearing the Big Blue," O'Hara said, referring to the Giants, "but I want you to know that I will always bleed Scarlet red." Apparently, Shaun felt he had deep roots in New Jersey's state university. In fact, one might even surmise that he is the original Scarlet O'Hara. In any case, Shaun O'Hara is an athlete who managed to make his sports dreams come true.

Shaun O'Hara–Courtesy Rutgers Athletic Communications

SHAQUILLE RASHAUN O'NEAL
Basketball
Newark, New Jersey
Born: March 6, 1972

He is one of New Jersey's biggest basketball stars, both in size and stature. He is a larger-than-life personality, blessed with big talent on and off of the basketball court. Shaquille O'Neal is not just a superb athlete who stands seven feet one inch tall and weighs in at 312 pounds, Shaq is also a gifted athlete and a highly regarded rap musician. His list of catchy nicknames is almost as long as the list of his personal achievements in sports. Shaquille has been known as "the Big Daddy," "the Real Deal," "the Big Aristotle," and "the Diesel." When O'Neal was traded to the Phoenix Suns in 2008, Shaq dubbed himself "the Big Cactus."

Phoenix Suns' star guard Steve Nash summed up the impact a player like Shaquille O'Neal has on a team. "He's charismatic, and he has a great personality," Nash said about his towering teammate.

Shaquille developed his unique and colorful personality during his youthful days as a self-described "military brat." He was born in Newark, New Jersey, but his family did not put down roots in the Garden State. Shaquille's dad was in the army. Shaq spent his boyhood growing up in army camps in New Jersey, Georgia, Germany, and Texas.

When he was thirteen years old, Shaquille was already six feet five inches tall. He was big, but undisciplined and uncoordinated as an athlete. His agility and strength had not yet caught up with his size. He tried baseball, football, and basketball early in high school, but failed to excel at any sports. He was even cut from his ninth-grade basketball squad.

Shaquille stuck to sports and improved enough to make the basketball team at Robert G. Cole Senior High School in San Antonio, Texas. O'Neal ended up averaging thirty-two points, twenty-two rebounds, and eight blocked shots per game.

Shaquille O'Neal wrote to Coach Dale Brown at Louisiana State University and told him he wanted to play basketball at LSU. Coach Brown was more than happy to oblige. Shaquille was accepted at LSU after he graduated from high school.

Shaquille spent three years as a star player for Coach Brown. LSU went 23–9 in 1990, 20–10 in 1991, and 21–10 in 1992. In 1991, sophomore Shaquille O'Neal led the nation in rebounds with 411 rebounds in twenty-eight games, for a 14.7 per-game average. He was the United Press International Division I Player of the Year and the winner of the Associated Press's Rupp Trophy as college basketball's best player. In 1992, LSU's Shaquille O'Neal led the country in blocked shots with 157 blocks in thirty games, for an average of 5.23 blocked shots per game.

In his three-year career at LSU, Shaquille blocked a total of 412 shots, averaging 4.58 blocks per game. He also averaged 21.6 points per game, shooting .575 from the floor. After his junior year, O'Neal decided to turn pro.

Shaquille O'Neal was the first player selected in the 1992 NBA draft. He was picked by the Orlando Magic and announced his arrival in the pro ranks in typical brash Shaquille O'Neal fashion. He won NBA Rookie of the Year honors by averaging 23.4 points per game and was named to the National Basketball Association's All-Star squad. It was to be the first of thirteen straight All-Star appearances for O'Neal.

Shaq continued his pro point parade in year two in the NBA. By the end of his second season, Shaquille O'Neal had scored a total of 4,270 points in 162 games for a per-game average of 26.4 points per contest. He'd also accumulated 2,194 rebounds and 517 blocked shots.

The Big Diesel kept rolling. In addition to the Orlando Magic, he played for the Los Angeles Lakers, the Miami Heat, and the Phoenix Suns. Along the way, he became a four-time NBA Champion. He was named the Most Valuable Player of the NBA Play-offs in 2000, 2001, and 2002. Shaquille O'Neal joined a small, elite group of basketball stars who were named both the College Player of the Year and the Most Valuable Player of the NBA.

In 2000, O'Neal led the National Basketball Association in scoring with 2,344 points, for an average of 29.7 points per game. In recognition of his great year, Shaq was awarded the Maurice Podoloff Trophy as the National Basketball Association's top player.

In 2002–03, Shaquille O'Neal tallied 1,841 points, for an average of 27.5 points per game. He also pulled down 742 rebounds and had 159 blocked shots.

Finally in 2007–08, injuries slowed Shaq's relentless point pace. For the first time since his rookie season, he failed to make the All-Star squad. A hip injury in the first half of the NBA season hampered Shaq's usual court production. His absence was duly noted with respect by his pro peers. All-Star Carmelo Anthony of the Denver Nuggets told reporters, "He's our godfather. It don't feel right without having him here."

The plain fact is Shaq will be back. He was slowed just a bit by age and injury, but his illustrious career is far from over. The man who poured in over twenty thousand career points in pro play announced to the press his intentions to win a fifth NBA crown before he hangs up his king-size sneakers. And Shaquille O'Neal usually accomplishes what he sets out to do!

NBA great Allen Iverson had this to say about Shaquille: "He's just a good guy on and off the floor," Iverson said at the 2008 NBA All-Star game. "He's the best there will ever be at that position."

DUANE CHARLES "BILL" PARCELLS

Football
Englewood, New Jersey
Born: August 22, 1941

His nickname is "the Tuna." It is a moniker hooked on him by the New England Patriots linebackers he coached as an NFL assistant in the early 1980s. Bill Parcells is a football coach well schooled in the *X*'s and *O*'s of pro football strategy. Teams evolve into championship squads under the direction of this magical gridiron mentor. There's no secret trick to the football successes of New Jersey's own Bill Parcells. It's just a matter of hard work, wise personal decisions, and superlative coaching methods.

Bill Parcells played high school football at River Dell Regional High School in Bergen Country, New Jersey. Parcells was a good-sized youngster and played linebacker at Wichita State University (formerly the University of Wichita) in Kansas. After graduation, Parcells bounced around as an assistant college coach at numerous schools.

Bill coached at Hastings (1964), Wichita State (1965), Army (1966–69), Florida State (1970–72), Vanderbilt (1973–74), and Texas Tech (1975–77). In 1978, Bill Parcells got his first job as a head football coach. He was hired to pilot the gridiron squad at the Air Force Academy in Colorado. He held that position for a single season.

In 1979, Parcells stepped up to the professional ranks and served as the defensive coordinator of the New York Giants under head coach Ray Perkins. The following season, he migrated north to the New England Patriots, where he picked up his famous nickname guiding linebackers for head coach Ron Erhardt. After a year in New England the well-traveled Bill Parcells returned to the Giants. At the conclusion of the 1982 NFL season, head coach Ray Perkins announced he was departing New York to take over the head-coaching duties at his college alma mater, the University of Alabama. George Young, the Giants' general manager, announced that Bill Parcells would take over as New York's head coach.

In 1983, Coach Parcells assumed the head-coaching duties of a team that had posted a single winning season in the previous ten years. The Giants were regarded as NFL bottom-feeders. Parcells was a great coach, but he was not a miracle worker. The Giants recorded a dismal record of three wins, twelve losses, and one tie his first year at the helm.

Football fans wondered if Bill Parcells was about to make a hasty exit from the NFL head-coaching ranks. The New York Giants wisely stood by their choice. The next year, Parcells guided the Giants to a 9–7 record, with some help from blossoming quarterback Phil Simms. The following season, New York won ten games and lost six contests. The Giants went to the NFL Play-offs two years in a row.

Parcells continued to build. He designed his offense around quarterback Phil Simms. He revamped the team defense of his squad He devised ways to utilize the unique defensive talents of a superb linebacking corps, which included Lawrence Taylor, Harry Carson, and Carl Banks.

The "new" New York Giants went 14–6 in 1986. The Giants topped the San Francisco 49ers and the Washington Redskins to capture the NFC crown and to advance to the Super Bowl. In Super Bowl XXI, Bill Parcells coached the Giants to a 39–20 victory over the Denver Broncos

Bill Parcells was named the UPI NFL Coach of the Year, the AP NFL Coach of the Year, and the Sporting News NFL Coach of the Year for 1986.

In 1990, the New York Giants won their first ten games of the season. The squad finished the year with thirteen wins and three losses. Parcells coached his Big Blue team to a thrilling come-from-behind victory over the San Francisco 49ers in the NFC championship game. A last-second field goal by Giants' kicker Matt Bahr gave New York a miraculous 15–13 victory.

Super Bowl XXV also turned into a gridiron nail-biter. The contest was an all-New York football clash, as the Giants took on the AFC champion Buffalo Bills. The Giants won the nerve-wracking matchup 20–19 when Buffalo placekicker Scott Norwood missed a last -gasp forty-seven-yard field-goal attempt.

Health problems prompted Bill Parcells to retire after the 1990 season. His accomplishments with the Giants were nothing less than spectacular. Under his guidance, New York won three division titles (1986, 1989, and 1990), two NFC championships (1986 and 1990), and two Super Bowls (XXI and XXV).

After working as a sports broadcaster and TV analyst for a few seasons, a healthy Bill Parcells returned to coaching in 1993. He was named head coach of the New England Patriots. Once again, Parcells had the magic touch when it came to righting a sinking gridiron ship. In 1994, the Tuna skippered the Pats to a record of ten wins and six losses. New England returned to the play-offs after a six-year absence. Parcells was named the Maxwell Football Club NFL Coach of the Year, the Associated Press NFL Coach of the Year, the Pro Football Weekly NFL Coach of the Year, and the United Press International Coach of the Year.

The New England Patriots captured an AFC conference Crown in 1996 and advanced to the Super Bowl. The Green Bay Packers defeated the New England Patriots 35–21 in Super Bowl XXXI, to keep Coach Bill Parcells from earning a third Super Bowl championship.

At the end of the season, Parcells was named the Pro Football Weekly NFL Coach of the Year for 1996. Bill Parcells left his head-coaching position with the Patriots in 1996 due to a dispute with management over who should control player personnel choices. Parcells wanted more power when it came to picking who would play for his team. In explaining the situation, Parcells came up with a classic line: "If they want you to cook the dinner, at least they ought to let you shop for some of the groceries."

Bill Parcells later served as the head coach of the New York Jets and the Dallas Cowboys. He did experience a degree of success in both places, but they did not match the banner years he experienced with the Giants and the Patriots.

Working with Bill Parcells has also become a training ground for future NFL head coaches. Former assistant coaches under Parcells who've gone on to guide NFL clubs include Tom Coughlin, Romeo Crennel, Bill Belichick, and several others.

DREW PEARSON
Football
South River, New Jersey
Born: January 12, 1951

Many outstanding wide receivers have played for the Dallas Cowboys, including Michael Irvin, Bob Hayes, and Tony Hill. Counted among the Cowboys' elite corps of pass catchers is a South River, New Jersey-born athlete who made a habit of working last-minute miracles on the pro gridiron.

Originally, Drew Pearson was a gifted field general, who played quarterback at South River High School in New Jersey. Pearson succeeded future NFL QB Joe Theismann after Theismann left to attend the University of Notre Dame. Pearson was a talented high school QB, but he realized his best chance of finding a home in the National Football League would be at another position.

Drew Pearson attended University of Tulsa after high school and switched from the quarterback position to wide receiver. Drew was a natural at his new position. He had good speed, great moves, and sure hands. Unfortunately, the University of Tulsa was a run-oriented team at the time, and Pearson only caught a total of thirty-three passes at his flanker position.

Drew Pearson graduated from Tulsa in 1972, but was not picked in the NFL draft. However, the Dallas Cowboys liked what they saw in the speedy receiver and quickly signed him to a free-agent contract. Drew made the team and rapidly developed into a remarkable wideout.

In the Cowboys' 1973 NFC Play-off game against the Los Angeles Rams, Pearson made a key catch for a touchdown that sealed Dallas' 27–16 victory. In 1974, Drew Pearson caught sixty-two passes for 1,087 yards and two touchdowns. He averaged 17.5 yards per catch. Pearson's gridiron efforts were rewarded with a berth on the 1974 All-Pro squad.

The 1975 season was the year Drew Pearson's pass-catching ability took on a mystical aura. The magic was worked with twenty-five seconds remaining in an NFC Play-off game between the Dallas Cowboys and the Minnesota Vikings. The Cowboys were trailing the Vikings by a score of 10–14. Dallas had the ball on the fifty-yard line with time for a last-gasp pass attempt. It would take a miracle to snatch victory from the jaws of defeat. Cowboys' center Kyle Davis made a shotgun snap to quarterback Roger Staubach. Staubach scrambled as he watched Drew Pearson streak down the field, battling Vikings' defensive back Nate Wright for position every step of the way.

With time running out, Staubach launched a long, high pass in the general direction of Pearson. The toss became known as a Hail Mary throw, because Dallas fans shut their eyes and prayed a Cowboy player would reel in the wayward pigskin. Miraculously, Drew Pearson answered that prayer. Somehow he managed to make the catch as the Vikings' defender tumbled to the turf. Pearson secured the pigskin and skipped into the end zone. Drew Pearson's miracle reception of a fifty-yard Hail Mary touchdown toss with time running out gave the Cowboys an astounding 17–14 victory over the Vikings. Pearson's amazing grab is rated as one of the greatest catches in NFL history.

In 1976, Drew Pearson led the National Football Conference with fifty-eight receptions (for 806 yards and six TDs). He was named All-Pro in 1976. Pearson repeated as an All-Pro performer in 1977, when he led the NFC in receiving yards with 870 yards. He made forty-eight catches and tallied two TDs that season. Drew Pearson had another great year in 1979. He snared fifty-five passes good for 1,026 yards and eight touchdowns.

In January of 1981, Pearson returned to working miracles on the gridiron. IThe miracle occurred in the second round of the NFC Play-offs against the Atlanta Falcons. Once again, Dallas was on the short end of a 27–24 score. There were fifty seconds left on the clock. The Cowboys had the ball on the Falcons' twenty-three-yard line. Cowboys' fans held their breath and prayed for another miracle. Danny White, the Cowboys' quarterback, fired a Hail Mary pass to Mr. Miracle, Drew Pearson. Pearson was double covered by Atlanta defenders Tom Pridemore and Rolland Lawrence. High up into the air went Drew Pearson, as if lifted by the wings of angels. To the disbelief of Falcons' players, fans, and coaches, down came Pearson with the pigskin cradled in his midsection. Drew Pearson had done it again! The Cowboys won 30–17 on a magical play that defied explanation.

Drew Pearson was named a captain of the Dallas Cowboys' squad in 1977, 1978, 1982, and 1983. He played in three Super Bowls and earned a Super Bowl championship ring in 1978 (Super Bowl XII) when Dallas defeated the Denver Broncos 27–10.

Pearson retired from pro football after the 1983 season. Over his career he caught 489 passes for 7,822 yards and forty-eight touchdowns. He also scored two touchdowns on fumble recoveries. Drew Pearson was named one of the Top 20 Pro Football All-Time Receivers and voted to the NFL 1970s All-Decade Team.

The name Drew Pearson will forever come to mind whenever pro-football fans cross their fingers, hold their breath, and pray for the miracle completion of a desperation Hail Mary pass.

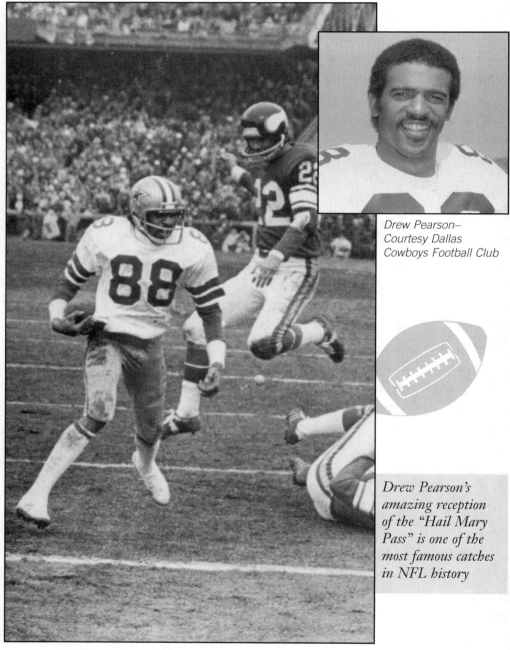

*Drew Pearson–
Courtesy Dallas
Cowboys Football Club*

Drew Pearson's amazing reception of the "Hail Mary Pass" is one of the most famous catches in NFL history

Drew Pearson–Courtesy Dallas Cowboys Football Club

RICHARD S. PROEHL
Football
Hillsborough, New Jersey
Born: March 7, 1968

Richard "Ricky" Proehl was born in the Bronx, New York, but grew up playing football and baseball in rural Hillsborough, New Jersey. Proehl was a gifted athlete, blessed with great hands and good speed. It was Ricky Proehl's uncanny ability to always make the crucial big catch that propelled him to stardom on the gridiron.

As a member of the Hillsborough High School Raiders football squad, young Ricky Proehl was a lanky speedster who ran precise pass routes and had sure hands. He seldom if ever dropped the ball. The pigskin seemed to stick to his fingers. As a senior, Proehl hauled in forty-two passes for over nine hundred yards and thirteen touchdowns. He was rewarded for a spectacular season on offense and defense by being named the Somerset County (New Jersey) High School Football Player of the Year. Proehl was voted First Team All-State. Ricky Proehl accepted a football scholarship to Wake Forest University and promptly became a starting wide receiver for the Demon Deacons.

Playing in the Atlantic Coast Conference suited the sure-handed ball catcher, and Proehl set several Wake Forest receiving records over his four-year varsity career. Ricky Proehl holds the Demon Deacons' record for receiving yards (2,949) and touchdowns scored (twenty-five). At the conclusion of his college career, Proehl appeared in the Blue-Gray Football Classic and the East-West All-Star Game.

Professional scouts were impressed with what they saw, and Ricky Proehl was selected by the Arizona Cardinals in the third round of the 1990 NFL draft. He was the fifty-eighth player picked. Proehl began a sixteen-year NFL career by leading the Cardinals in receptions his rookie season.

Hillsborough's Ricky Proehl enjoys the distinction of being the first football star from Somerset County, New Jersey, to play in four Super Bowls (with three different teams). In all, Proehl played for six National Football League teams. He was a member of the Arizona Cardinals from 1990 to 1994. Proehl was on the Seattle Seahawks from 1995 to 1996. Ricky Proehl spent the 1997 season reeling in passes for the Chicago Bears. In 1998, Proehl found a football home with the Saint Louis Rams. He remained with the Rams for four seasons. In the 1999 NFC championship tilt, which matched Saint Louis against the Tampa Bay Buccaneers, Ricky Proehl lived up to his gridiron billing as a clutch pass catcher. The Rams were trailing the Buccaneers with four minutes and forty-four seconds to go in the game when Proehl made a key grab for the go-ahead touchdown. Saint Louis defeated Tampa Bay 11–6, and the Rams punched their ticket to the Super Bowl with a little help from their go-to guy, Ricky Proehl. On the day Proehl pulled in six receptions for one hundred yards, coach Dick Vermeil's Rams went on to best the Tennessee Titans 23–16 in Super Bowl XXXIV.

Two years later, the Saint Louis Rams and their clutch receiver, Ricky Proehl, returned to the Super Bowl championship game to butt heads against the New England Patriots. The Rams were losing 17 –10 with only one minute and thirty seconds to play. Proehl made another miracle touchdown catch to tie the contest. However, a last-gasp field goal by Patriots' kicker, Adam Vinatieri, gave New England a 20–17 victory.

Ricky Proehl performed his NFL pass-catching duties for the Carolina Panthers from 2003 to 2005. In Super Bowl XXXVIII, Proehl, as a member of the Panthers, once again had a chance to shine against the AFC champion New England Patriots. With a little over a minute to go in the contest, Proehl once again snared a key touchdown pass to knot the game at 29 all. The clutch catch proved to be for naught as New England kicker Adam Vinatieri again spoiled Proehl's amazing performance by booting a last tick field goal to ice a 32–29 Patriot victory.

Star wide receiver Ricky Proehl finally got a second Super Bowl ring as a member of the 2006 World Champion Indianapolis Colts.

Proehl's career stats as a pro receiver are impressive. Sure-handed Ricky Proehl had 669 pass receptions good for 8,878 yards and fifty-four touchdowns. He will be best remembered as a pro receiver who always made the clutch catch-es.

Ricky Proehl–Courtesy Indianapolis Colts Football

WILLIS REED
Basketball
Cedar Grove, New Jersey
Born: June 25, 1942

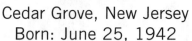

Willis Reed was born in Hico, Louisiana, and grew up on a farm in Bernice, Louisiana. Young Willis eventually grew into a six foot ten inch, 235-pound center who had a strong inside game and a deadly short-range jump shot.

Reed took his game to Grambling State University and became an instant court sensation. Willis Reed led Grambling to three Southwestern Athletic Conference Championships and a National Association of Intercollegiate Athletics (NAIA) basketball championship in 1961. Reed scored 2,280 points over his college career and was a small-college All-American in 1963, his senior year.

The New York Knicks picked Willis Reed in the second round of the 1964 NBA draft. Reed wasted no time in making his presence felt on NBA courts as a rookie. In March of 1965, he scored forty-six points against the powerful Los Angeles Lakers. Willis Reed had a dynamite rookie year for the Knicks in 1965. He exploded for 1,560 points, pulled down 1,175 rebounds, and had 133 assists. He averaged 19.5 points and 14.7 rebounds per game. Willis Reed was named an NBA All-Star and selected as the Rookie of the Year in the National Basketball Association.

Over the next ten NBA seasons, Willis Reed became a mainstay in the middle for the New York Knickerbockers. He starred at center (and briefly at forward) while providing leadership and inspiration for his teammates. He soon was dubbed "the Captain" and eventually became the Knicks' official team captain.

From 1966 to 1971, Willis Reed averaged over twenty points per game as a member of the New York Knicks. His best point productions were in 1968–69, when he tallied a total of 1,733 points for a 21.1 points per game average and in 1969–70, when Reed scored 1,755 total points for a 21.7 points per game average. In a 1969 contest against the Detroit Pistons, Reed poured in forty-eight points in a 135–87 New York victory.

The New York Knicks, led by "the Captain" Willis Reed, went on a tear during the 1969–70 season. The Knicks won sixty games and had an eighteen-game winning streak. They roared into the NBA Championship Series and were matched against the powerful Los Angles Lakers. The series was a hard-fought seesaw battle. The tide of momentum continued to shift until the series was tied at three games apiece. The seventh and deciding game set the stage for Willis Reed's most famous NBA appearance.

Willis Reed had suffered a severe and painful leg injury during championship play. He was unable to appear on the floor in game six of the title series. His absence gave the Lakers a huge advantage. No one expected Willis Reed to play in the final court contest to determine the NBA champion. However, the Knicks' captain refused to be sidelined. He gritted his teeth, ignored the pain, and limped out onto the basketball court in New York's Madison Square Garden to face his foes. The fans on hand went wild. They roared their approval and loudly voiced their admiration for the Knicks' captain. Reed only scored four points in the contest and eventually couldn't continue to participate, but his appearance inspired his teammates to excel beyond any normal expectations. New York guard Walt Frazier scored thirty-six points in leading the Knicks to a 113–99 victory. New York won its first NBA Championship.

Willis Reed was named the NBA's regular-season MVP, and also the Most Valuable Player of the NBA Play-offs. It was the first time in NBA history one player had captured both awards.

Injuries continued to plague the Knicks' captain over the remainder of his career. However, in 1972–73, Willis Reed led the Knicks to their second NBA championship. Once again, New York bested the Los Angeles Lakers to secure the title. This time the championship series went only five games. Willis Reed was named the Most Valuable Player of the 1973 NBA Play-offs.

Nagging injuries hastened the retirement of the Knicks' captain. Reed retired after the 1973–74 NBA season.

Willis Reed spent his entire pro career with the New York Knicks. Reed scored a total of 12,183 points and yanked down 8,414 rebounds. He also dished out 1,186 assists. In play-off action, Willis Reed tallied 1,358 points and pulled in 801 rebounds. Reed was named an NBA All-Star seven straight times (1965 to 1971).

After his playing days ended, Willis Reed coached with the New York Knicks, the Sacramento Kings, the Atlanta Hawks, and the New Jersey Nets. He also coached at Creighton University. In 2008, Reed worked in basketball operations for the New Orleans Hornets.

Willis Reed was elected to the Basketball Hall of Fame in 1981. His number (nineteen) was retired by the New York Knickerbockers in 1976. Knick fans will always remember Willis Reed as "the Captain" who played through the pain and helped New York win its first NBA championship.

Wills Reed has made Cedar Grove, New Jersey, his home base for many years.

JAMES S. RINGO
Football
Orange, New Jersey
Born: November 21, 1931

Fame, fortune, and success never changed him. Football hero Jim Ringo will always be remembered by those who knew him best as just a regular guy with simple tastes.

However, on a football field, there was nothing ordinary or mundane about Jim Ringo's style of play. Ringo epitomized the determined, hard-nosed qualities and game intelligence necessary to become a Hall of Fame offensive center. He was also a quiet team leader who eventually evolved into a consummate line coach.

Jim Ringo was born in Orange, New Jersey, but grew up in Phillipsburg, New Jersey, a stone's throw from the Pennsylvania border. Ringo played football for Phillipsburg High, and played it well enough to earn a scholarship to Syracuse University, where he was coached by gridiron immortal Ben Schwartzwalder.

In the 1953 NFL draft, center Jim Ringo was the seventy-ninth player selected. He was picked by the Green Bay Packers in the seventh round. When Jim Ringo reported to the Packers' training camp, he was stunned by the gigantic size of the other offensive linemen. Ringo, who weighed in at only 211 pounds, was one of the smallest guys there. Nevertheless, Jim Ringo's agility, quickness, and flawless blocking techniques helped him to rapidly rise to the top of head coach Gene Ronzani's depth chart. When coach Lisle Blackbourn took over the Packers' reins the following year (1954), Ringo was already a budding star blocker in the middle of the offensive line. Jim was a Pro Bowl selection by 1957, which was Blackbourn's final season as the Green Bay coach. With Coach Ray McClean at the helm, Jim Ringo was once again a Pro Bowl selection in 1958. By then, the undersized pro center had beefed up to a robust 235 pounds, which was still light for an NFL lineman. When Vince Lombardi took over the Green Bay Packers in 1959, Jim Ringo found he was a perfect fit for the Packers' new style run to daylight Lombardi offense.

Coach Vince Lombardi was an advocate of the power sweep. He liked swift, mobile blockers who could pull out of the line and race around the corner to lead interference for ball carriers. Jim Ringo fit that blocking assignment perfectly. Ringo's contribution to the Packers' new success under Coach Vince Lombardi was not overlooked by his peers in the pro ranks. Ringo was named an All-Pro every year from 1959 to 1963. The Green Bay Packers won the NFL championship crowns in 1961 and 1962.

Years later, Packers linebacker Dave Robinson described Ringo's contribution to the Green Bay squad this way: "You could tell he was a leader . . . not just an offensive leader, but a team leader." Leadership to Jim Ringo meant being out on the field game after grueling game. He was remarkably resilient for a small player in a brutal game where bumps, bruises, and injuries frequently removed even the most rugged athletes from the lineup. Jim Ringo started every Packer football game from 1954 to 1963.

In 1964, Coach Vince Lombardi traded Jim Ringo to the Philadelphia Eagles. Some say Lombardi made the surprise move because Ringo brought in an agent to negotiate a raise. Others claim Lombardi made the trade to secure the Eagles' first-round pick in the draft. Whatever the case, Jim Ringo moved to Philadelphia and became the Eagles' star center. He played for the Eagles from 1964 to 1967 and was a Pro Bowl selection three times (1964, 1965, and 1967).

Ringo retired after the 1967 season. As a pro, he'd started 182 consecutive NFL games. Jim Ringo was selected to the Pro Bowl ten times, and voted All-NFL seven times.

Jim Ringo was successful and famous, but he never forgot his roots in the Garden State. He made frequent visits to his hometown of Phillipsburg, New Jersey, during his playing career.

After his retirement as an active player, Jim Ringo remained in the pro ranks as a coach. He served as an assistant coach with the Buffalo Bills, the Chicago Bears, the New England Patriots, and the New York Jets. When head coach Lou Saban resigned from the Buffalo Bills early in 1976, Jim Ringo took over the squad. It was the only season Ringo spent as a head coach in the NFL.

Center Jim Ringo was named to the NFL 1960s All-Decade Team. In 1981, he was voted into the Pro Football Hall of Fame. When Ringo learned he'd been so honored, Jim humbly replied, "Who would've ever thought a kid from Phillipsburg, New Jersey, would make the Hall of Fame?" Jim Ringo, the regular guy with simple tastes, made the Pro Football Hall of Fame because he was a great NFL athlete who deserved the honor. When it came to playing offensive center, former Green Bay teammate Willie Davis summed up Jim Ringo's body of work in simple but glowing terms. "Probably no one was better," said Davis.

Jim Ringo died on November 19, 2007, at the age of seventy-five. He is buried at Fairmount Cemetery in New Jersey. Fairmount is a fitting place of eternal rest for football star Jim Ringo. Fairmount Cemetery is located in Ringo's beloved hometown of Phillipsburg, New Jersey.

Jim Ringo—Courtesy Syracuse University Athletics

PAUL ROBESON
Football
Princeton, New Jersey
Born: April 9, 1898

Paul Robeson was one of New Jersey's greatest all-around athletes. However, Robeson was much more than a sports star. He was a brilliant scholar, a gifted singer and performer, and a staunch advocate of equal rights.

Paul Robeson was born in Princeton, New Jersey. He was one of five children. Robeson's father had escaped from slavery in North Carolina and studied theology at Lincoln University in Pennsylvania. He became a Presbyterian minister.

The Robeson family moved from Princeton, New Jersey, to Union County, New Jersey, and eventually to Somerset County in central New Jersey. Paul Robeson grew up in Somerville, New Jersey, and attended Somerville High School, where he excelled in athletics, academics, and music. Paul Robeson was honored as his class valedictorian and received an academic scholarship to Rutgers, The State University of New Jersey. Robseon was the third African American student to be accepted to Rutgers. Paul entered Rutgers in 1915 and discovered he was the only African American student on campus.

Robeson began his stellar athletic career at Rutgers as a member of coach George Foster Sanford's gridiron squad. Sanford would later be inducted into the College Football Hall of Fame. Paul Robeson joined All-American Bob "Nasty" Nash in leading Rutgers to an impressive record of seven wins and one loss in 1915. Robeson was quickly hailed as one of Rutgers's rising stars, but Paul never let instant fame affect his personality.

"Everybody liked him," said Walter Steward, a classmate of Robeson's in a newspaper interview years later. "He was never arrogant or anything of that sort."

In 1916, Paul Robeson was one of a select few African Americans to star for a college team on the gridiron. Another was Fred "Fritz" Pollard, who was an All-American at Brown University. Paul Robeson played end on offense and linebacker on defense for Rutgers. Pollard and Robeson butted heads in a gridiron clash between Brown University and Rutgers University in 1916. Brown won the game by a score of 21–3. The game was most memorable because it pitted two of college football's earliest African American football heroes against each other.

In 1917, Paul Robeson won national acclaim as one of America's top college football stars. Rutgers finished the season with a record of seven wins, one loss, and one tie. Football icon Walter Camp said Paul Robeson "was the greatest to ever trot the gridiron".

Paul Robeson was named a First Team All-American in 1917. He repeated as a First Team All-American football player in 1918. Robeson was the first African American athlete to be named a First Team All-American football player in successive years.

Paul Robeson was not just a one-sport sensation while at Rutgers. He won a total of fifteen letters in football, baseball, basketball, and track. He graduated as class valedictorian. Robeson was also Phi Beta Kappa and was inducted into the Rutgers honor society, known as Cap and Skull.

Paul Robeson played several years of pro football after graduation. He also attended law school at the same time. Paul Robeson played end for the professional team known as the Akron (Ohio) Pros in 1920 and 1921. Other members of that squad included Rutgers's tackle Bob "Nasty" Nash and Brown University running back Fred "Fritz" Pollard. In 1920, the Akron Pros were unbeaten in ten games. Over the course of two seasons, Akron won fifteen games in a row and held thirteen opponents scoreless.

Paul Robeson also played professional football for the Hammond (Indiana) Pros and the Milwaukee (Wisconsin) Badgers. Early pro-football stars included Jim Thorpe, George Halas, and Curly Lambeau.

In 1923, Paul Robeson graduated from Columbia Law School. A member of his graduating class was future U.S. Supreme Court justice William O. Douglas.

Robeson then embarked upon a singing and theatrical career. He starred in *Othello* and the musical *Showboat*. Paul Robeson played the lead role in Eugene O'Neill's famous play *The Emperor Jones*. He also appeared in several movies.

Over the years, Paul Robeson garnered numerous awards for his tireless work for human rights. He was recognized by the New York Urban League and the American Civil Liberties Union for his many contributions to the equal rights movement. In 1983, East Germany honored Paul Robeson for his work combating racism by issuing a postage stamp bearing his likeness. In 1995, Paul Robeson was inducted into the College Football Hall of Fame.

Paul Robeson–Courtesy Rutgers Athletic Communications

MIKE ROZIER
Football
Camden, New Jersey
Born: March 1, 1961

Star halfback Mike Rozier was born to run. Rozier starred in football, basketball, and track at New Jersey's Woodrow Wilson High School. After a spectacular high school sports career, the Camden native accepted a football scholarship to play for coach Tom Osborne at the University of Nebraska.

The Nebraska Cornhuskers were a perennial college football powerhouse in the Big Eight Football Conference. During those years, Mike Rozier's uncanny rushing abilities added speed and balance to the awesome Nebraska offense. In 1984, Rozier helped the Huskers post a record of nine wins and three losses. Nebraska ended up ranked number eleven in the country after a tough 15–22 loss to Clemson in the Orange Bowl.

In 1982, the Cornhuskers went twelve and one with Mike Rozier leading the offensive assault. Nebraska defeated LSU 21–20 in the Orange Bowl, and finished the year ranked number three in the nation.

Mike Rozier's final season in the Big Eight Conference was his banner bon voyage to college football. Nebraska finished the regular season unbeaten with twelve wins. The Cornhuskers took on the Miami Hurricanes in the Orange Bowl in a gridiron contest to determine the national champion. In a fantastic football clash, Miami edged Nebraska 31–30 to capture the national crown. Nebraska ended up ranked number two in the country.

However, the Cornhuskers' best back, Mike Rozier, was second to none on a national level. Rozier led the nation in rushing. Mike carried the ball 275 times for 2,148 yards. He averaged 179 yards per game. Nebraska's Mike Rozier also topped all college backs in scoring in 1983. Rozier tallied twenty-nine touchdowns for a total of 174 points.

In his three-year career at Nebraska, Mike Rozier rushed for 4,780 yards on 668 carries. He averaged 7.2 yards per carry. Rozier also scored forty-eight touchdowns during his career. He had twenty-six games where he rushed for one hundred yards or more, and seven games where he rushed for two hundred yards or more.

Camden's Mike Rozier concluded his illustrious college-football career by winning both the Heisman Trophy and the Maxwell Award as college football's best player. In taking the Heisman Trophy, running back Mike Rozier bested quarterbacks Steve Young of Brigham Young University, who finished second, and Doug Flutie of Boston College, who finished third.

After college, Mike Rozier opted to play in the new United States Football League rather than the National Football League. He signed with the Pittsburgh Maulers of the USFL. In his second season in the new league, he jumped to the Jacksonville Bulls, where he rushed for 1,320 yards. When the USFL went bankrupt, Mike Rozier signed with the Houston Oilers of the National Football League. He played for the Oilers from 1985 to 1990. Rozier's best NFL season was in 1988, when he rushed for 1,002 yards and tallied ten touchdowns.

Mike Rozier, the halfback born to run, closed out his pro career as a member of the Atlanta Falcons, a team he joined in 1990. Rozier retired in 1991. During his eight-year NFL career, he was named a Pro Bowl selection two times (1987 and 1988). In all, Rozier carried the pigskin as an NFL pro player for 4,462 total yards. He also scored thirty touchdowns. In 2006, the ex-Nebraska star was voted into the College Football Hall of Fame.

GREGORY E. SCHIANO
Football
Wyckoff, New Jersey
Born: June 1, 1966

Greg Schiano left no doubts about his goal when he returned to his home state of New Jersey in December of 2000 to become the head football coach at Rutgers University. "We came here to build a program that will win national championships," Schiano boldly stated to the press and public. The brash prediction for the future of Rutgers football seemed far-fetched at the time. However, as gridiron seasons rolled past, Schiano's loftly goal rapidly became a distinct possibility. Rutgers eventually emerged from the shadows of college football and now basks in the glow of a national spotlight thanks to the expert guidance of a head coach born and raised in the Garden State.

Greg Schiano was born in Wyckoff, New Jersey, and played high school football at Ramapo High. After graduation, Schiano attended Bucknell University, where he starred as a linebacker. In 1986, junior linebacker Greg Schiano made 114 tackles and earned All-Conference honors. Schiano was named to the Sporting News All-America Preseason Team as a senior. He was also voted team captain of the Bucknell squad.

Greg Schiano moved on to the NFL trials after graduation, but watched in bitter disappointment as his dream of a professional-football career evaporated. Determined to make the sport of football his life's work, Schiano turned to coaching. In 1988, he was an assistant football coach at Ramapo High School. In 1989, he served as a graduate assistant football coach at Rutgers University. From 1990 to 1996, he coached at Penn State, first as a graduate assistant, and later as the coach of defensive backs.

Greg Schiano shifted gears and accepted a coaching position in the NFL in 1996. Greg was a defensive assistant coach for the Chicago Bears until 1997.

Greg Schiano's next coaching assignment was in the sunny state of Florida. Schiano returned to the college ranks as the defensive coordinator for the University of Miami Hurricanes. He remained at Miami until accepting the head-coaching position at Rutgers. Greg Schiano methodically retooled the gridiron machinery at one of college football's oldest institutions. In 2005, Schiano's transformation of the Garden State squad became apparent. The Rutgers Scarlet Knights posted a regular-season record of seven wins and five losses, and were invited to play in the Insight Bowl, located in Phoenix, Arizona. It was Rutgers's first bowl bid since 1978. Rutgers lost a 40–45 thriller to Arizona State in the Insight Bowl.

The very next year, Rutgers exploded on the national football scene. The Rutgers Scarlet Knights upset the number-three ranked Louisville Cardinals in a game nationally televised by ESPN. The Scarlet Knights posted a regular-season record of ten wins and two losses. Rutgers was invited to play against Kansas State in the first Texas Bowl, in Houston, Texas. Rutgers blasted Kansas State 37–10 to record its eleventh win of the 2006 season. The Scarlet Knights ended up ranked number twelve in the country.

Coach Greg Schiano was named the Home Depot National Coach of the Year in 2006. He was also honored as the National Coach of the Year by the Walter Camp Football Foundation and voted the Big East Coach of the Year. In addition, Rutgers's head football coach, Greg Schiano, was the winner of the prestigious Liberty Mutual Coach of the Year Award, which honors the nation's top college-football coach who best exemplifies responsibility and excellence on and off the field.

Coach Schiano's Scarlet Knights continued their winning ways in 2007. Rutgers posted a record of eight wins and five losses, which included a 52–30 victory over Ball State in the International Bowl in Toronto, Canada.

Greg Schiano has not only coached his Rutgers team into the national spotlight, he has also managed to showcase the individual talents of Rutgers players who aspired to play in the National Football League.

"He not only gets his team ready for Saturdays, he's getting his players ready to play on Sundays, as well," said former Scarlet Knight Shaun O'Hara, who won a Super Bowl championship with the New York Giants in 2008.

Indeed, Coach Greg Schiano has prepped many of his college stars for eventual pro-football careers. NFL stars Schiano has mentored include Nate Jones (Dallas Cowboys), Jeremy ZUTTAH (Tampa Bay Buccaneers), Cam Stephenson (Green Bay Packers), Darnell Stapleton (Pittsburgh Steelers), L. J. Smith (Philadelphia Eagles), Gary Brackett (Indianapolis Colts), Brian Leonard (Saint Louis Rams), and Rutgers's all-time leading ground gainer—Ray Rice (Baltimore Ravens).

Rutgers's head football coach Greg Schiano is a man whose actions speak louder than his words. When it comes to winning college football games, he is not a coach who makes idle boasts. When he sets a goal, it's just a matter of time before he reaches it.

Greg Schiano–Courtesy Patti Banks/Rutgers Athletic Communications

PHILLIP M. SIMMS
Football
Franklin Lakes, New Jersey
Born: November 3, 1955

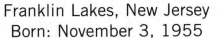

Phillip Martin Simms was born on his grandparents' farm in Washington County, Kentucky. Before he graduated from elementary school, Phil's family moved to Louisville, Kentucky, which is where he grew up. Former New York Giants quarterback Phil Simms now calls Franklin Lakes, New Jersey, his family home.

Phil Simms spent his college days playing quarterback for Morehead State University in Kentucky. Morehead State's gridiron squad was not considered a national powerhouse. In fact, the football team won only two games in Simms's senior year as a signal caller. In addition, Morehead State's offense utilized a grind-it-out running attack rather than a wide-open aerial game. Phil Simms's collegiate passing stats were good, but not great. Simms completed 409 passes in 835 attempts for 5,545 yards and thirty-two touchdowns during his college career. Nevertheless, pro scouts were very impressed with the young quarterback's physical attributes. He was highly regarded by a number of teams in the National Football League and was projected as a second- or third-round draft choice.

New York Giant football fans were stunned and shocked when their team made Morehead State quarterback Phil Simms their number one pick in the 1979 NFL draft. In fact, they loudly booed the Giants' choice.

Phil Simms quickly quieted the fans' unrest by showing flashes of brilliance in his rookie season. New York's young field general was victorious in the first five starts he made for the Giants. New York finished with a season record of six wins and ten losses in 1979, but with Simms behind center, the Giants were six and four. As a rookie, Phil threw for 1,743 yards and thirteen touchdowns. His effort earned him a berth on the All-NFL Rookie Squad.

Unfortunately, head coach Ray Perkins and quarterback Phil Simms didn't have the proper spark to jump-start the Giants' sputtering offense in 1980. New York posted a dismal league record of four wins and twelve losses. Simms passed for 2,321 yards and fifteen touchdowns, but also had nineteen interceptions. The 1981 season showed some improvement as New York posted a record of nine wins and seven losses. Phil Simms aired out the pigskin for 2,031 yards and eleven touchdowns before a shoulder separation sidelined him for the rest of the season.

Scott Brunner, New York's backup QB, stepped behind center and guided the Giants into the NFC Play-offs. New York, with Brunner calling the shots, beat the Philadelphia Eagles 27–21 in the first round of the play-offs and then lost to the San Francisco 49ers 24–38 in the second round. In 1982, Phil Simms tore a knee ligament in a preseason game and was lost for the year.

Once again, Scott Brunner took charge of the offense. This time the Giants sputtered through the season, backsliding to a four-and-six campaign. At the conclusion of the 1982 season, coach Ray Perkins left the Giants, and assistant coach Bill Parcells was elevated to the top job.

The following year, coach Bill Parcells elevated Scott Brunner to the position of starting quarterback over Phil Simms. Simms was assigned to bench duty.

When Phil Simms finally did get a chance to play, he once again suffered a season-ending injury. The Giants stumbled through another horrible year and won only three of twelve games.

The Giants seemed to be in a deep downward spiral. Fans wondered if the new head coach and the highly prized quarterback from Kentucky were a couple of flash-in-the-pan football flops.

Suddenly, the tide turned in 1984. Coach Bill Parcells and quarterback Phil Simms clicked and combined to lead the Giants to a 9–7 season and a play-off berth.

Phil Simms bounced back with a vengeance in 1985. He guided his Giants to a record of ten wins and six losses by passing for 3,829 yards and twenty-two touchdowns. On October 13, 1985, in a game against the Cincinnati Bengals, Giants quarterback Phil Sims completed forty passes for an amazing total of 513 yards!

The Giants' super signal caller was named to the Pro Bowl, which was played on February 2, 1986, in Honolulu, Hawaii. Phil Simms earned MVP honors in the 1986 Pro Bowl by tossing three TD passes and leading the NFC All-Stars to a 28–24 comeback victory over the AFC All-Stars.

The 1986 NFL season was Phil Simms's stepping-stone to lasting gridiron stardom. The Giants won fourteen regular-season contests and lost only two games. In the NFC Play-offs, they beat the San Francisco 49ers 49–3 and the Washington Redskins 17–0. The New York Giants took on the Denver Broncos in Super Bowl XXI.

Super Bowl XXI turned out to be a Phil Simms highlight reel. It was one of the most dazzling performances every recorded by a pro quarterback in a championship contest. Before the game began, Phil Simms told his teammates, "I got it today."

On the Giants' first offensive possession, Simms drove the Giants seventy-eight yards for a score by connecting on six straight passes. The TD toss that capped the march was a six-yard strike to tight end Zeke Mowatt.

Sims completed twelve of fifteen passes in the first half, good for 102 yards, but Denver led at the break by a 10–9 score.

In the second half, the confident Giants' quarterback took over the game. Simms completed ten straight passes at one point. He connected on touchdown strikes to tight end Mark Bavaro (thirteen yards) and wideout Phil McConkey (six yards). The Giants added two touchdown runs and a field goal to best the Denver Broncos by a 39–20 score. Phil Simms was named the Most Valuable Player of Super Bowl XXI. He completed twenty-two of twenty-five passes for 268 yards and three touchdowns. Simms also rushed three times for twenty-five yards. Phil's phenomenal performance was an exclamation-point answer to those impulsive Giants' fans who had booed his selection at the NFL draft many years earlier.

In 1990, Phil Simms was leading the Giants to another Super Bowl appearance when he suffered a broken foot after guiding his Big Blue team to eleven wins in fourteen games. Backup QB Jeff Hostetler took the Giants' team the rest of the way, which included a 20–19 win in Super Bowl XXV.

Quarterback Phil Simms retired in 1993 after starting all sixteen games for the Giants and leading the Big Blue to a record of eleven wins and five losses. Phil Simms spent his entire fourteen-year NFL career with one team—the New York Giants. He completed 2,576 passes in 4,647 attempts for 33,462 yards and 199 touchdowns. Simms also rushed for 1,252 yards and tallied six TDs. Phil Simms's number eleven has been retired by the New York Giants. Simms now works as a football analyst and sports broadcaster.

Phil Simms–Courtesy Morehead State Athletic Media Relations

DAVID JOEL STERN
Basketball
Teaneck, New Jersey
Born: September 22, 1942

Every sports fan knows basketball is a five-person game. A perfect combination can produce astounding results in the game of basketball. To net success, each person must make a special and unique contribution to the game. In the 1984–85 NBA season, five extremely gifted and talented individuals made dazzling debuts in the high-profile world court of professional basketball. Each one in his own way helped elevate the game of professional hoops to new and admirable heights.

The first member of that fab five was Utah Jazz rookie John Stockton. Over his career, Stockton would quietly amass over three thousand steals and over fifteen thousand assists. The second member of that super squad was an individual not known for quiet accomplishments. Philadelphia 76er Charles Barkley loudly announced his NBA presence by going on to tally over twenty-three thousand career points. The third member of the dream crew was the Houston Rockets' Hakeem "the Dream" Olajuwan, who scored over twenty-six thousand points and blocked over 3,800 shots.

The rising star with the brightest court future who entered the NBA spotlight in 1984–85 was young Michael Jordan. The Chicago Bulls' rookie would eventually score over thirty-two thousand points, make over 2,500 steals, and capture ten NBA scoring titles.

Stockton, Barkley, Olajuwan and Jordan are members of the NBA's 50 Greatest Players Ever squad. The fifth and final member of that dazzling rookie group of 1984–85 has also accomplished great things in his NBA tenure. Even though he is not a player, he is a key individual who helps set the course for the NBA and pilots the league through professional sports waters, both troubled and calm. He is David J. Stern, the man who became the commissioner of the National Basketball Association on February 1, 1984.

David Stern was born in New York City, but grew up in Teaneck, New Jersey. Stern attended Teaneck High School, where he excelled in academics. David's outstanding classroom accomplishments earned him a full scholarship to Rutgers, The State University of New Jersey. Stern was a dean's-list student and graduated from Rutgers College in 1963. David Stern then pursued a law degree and attended Columbia Law School in New York. Stern graduated in 1966 and began a long and illustrious association with the National Basketball Association. In 1966, Stern served as an outside counsel for the NBA. David Stern was drafted by the NBA in 1978 and picked to serve as the league's general counsel. Stern's NBA role steadily increased in importance due to his many key contributions. In 1980, Stern became the league's executive vice president.

During that period, Stern was involved in decisions that helped reshape the image and direction of the NBA. He was part of landmark settlements between the NBA and players that led to free agency. He was involved in the agreement that led to the salary cap and to revenue sharing. David Stern also had a hand in the creation of NBA Entertainment, a multimedia, television, and marketing company that promotes the league.

Finally, in 1984, David Stern was unanimously elected the NBA's fourth commissioner. With Stern in charge, the National Basketball Association continued to expand its horizons both nationally and internationally. The NBA added six new franchises. Two of those franchises were located in Canadian cities. In 1988, the National Basketball Association added the Charlotte Hornets and the Miami Heat. The Minnesota Timberwolves and the Orlando Magic entered the NBA in 1989. In 1995, the Toronto Raptors and the Vancouver (now Memphis) Grizzlies joined the NBA. In 2002, the Hornets moved to New Orleans, and in 2004, the Charlotte Bobcats became the sixth team to enter the NBA during David Stern's impressive reign as commissioner.

The National Basketball Association actively pursued a global fan base and market. As time marched on, NBA games were televised in over two hundred countries. More and more international hoop stars were scouted and signed by NBA teams. The National Basketball Association set up training camps in foreign countries and played exhibition games around the world. NBA offices have been established in numerous cities outside the U.S. Commissioner Stern's vision for the future growth of the NBA seems to know no boundaries.

The Women's National Basketball Association (WNBA), which is owned and operated by the NBA, has slowly increased in popularity since the league began play in 1997. The WNBA was created during Stern's ongoing term as commissioner.

However, marketing victories and sports business successes are not the only causes of concern to the commissioner. Under David Stern's insightful guidance, the NBA's charitable contributions have also increased. The National Basketball Association supports the NBA's Read To Achieve and NBA Cares social programs.

Mr. David Stern has held prestigious positions on numerous boards, including being the chair emeritus of the trustees of Columbia University. Mr. Stern is in the Rutgers University Hall of Distinguished Alumni. In 1999, NBA Commissioner David Stern was inducted into the Sports Hall of Fame of New Jersey.

Just like John Stockton, Charles Barkley, Hakeem Olajuwan, Michael Jordan, and others, David Stern's many contributions to the game of pro basketball have made him a NBA immortal.

David Stern–Courtesy NBA Entertainment

C. VIVIAN STRINGER
Basketball
Princeton, New Jersey
Born: March 16, 1948

There is no mystery concerning the meteoric rise of the Rutgers women's basketball program. It can be attributed to the tireless and innovative coaching and recruiting efforts of head coach C. Vivian Stringer.

Coach Stringer is certainly no mysterious miracle worker. She is an intense court mentor who demands offensive and especially defensive perfection from her players. Optimum effort is always expected. However, Coach Stringer is not all take and no give. She is loyally devoted to her players and wants them to succeed not only on the basketball court, but out in the real world, as well. Stringer thinks of her team as her family.

C. Vivian Stringer has accumulated over eight hundred hard-earned hoop victories in her years of coaching at Cheyney University, the University of Iowa, and Rutgers, The State University of New Jersey. Coach Stringer is also the only person to have guided three different schools to the NCAA Women's Basketball Tournament Final Four. How Stringer accomplished her Herculean hoop feats is no mystery. There is nothing mysterious about basketball icon C. Vivian Stringer. Then again, there may be one small secret to reveal. The *C* in C. Vivian Stringer stands for Charlene. Mystery solved.

C. Vivian Stringer was born in Edenborn, Pennsylvania, and excelled on the basketball court as a guard. She attended Slippery Rock University in Pennsylvania and graduated in 1970. She completed her master's degree in health and physical education in 1973. C. Vivian Stringer began her coaching career at Cheyney State (now Cheyney University) in 1971–72. Cheyney is a small school outside the city of Brotherly Love. From 1971 to 1982, Coach Stringer awed hoop fans with her innovative style of women's basketball, which stressed pressure defense. The small Pennsylvania school near Philadelphia developed a national reputation as an eastern power in women's basketball. When the NCAA sponsored its first-ever national tournament in 1982, Coach C. Vivian Stringer and her Cheyney Wolves battled their way into the championship game against Louisiana Tech. Louisiana Tech, coached by Sonya Hogg, topped Coach C. Vivian Stringer's Cheyney club by a score of 76–62 to win the national title.

In 1979, Cheyney was ranked ninth in the country. Cheyney enjoyed another great year in 1981 and was ranked fifth in the nation. In 1982, the Cheyney Wolves finished as America's number-two team. C. Vivian Stringer was honored by being awarded the 1982 NCAA Wade Trophy for the national coach of the year. Coach Stringer's career record at Cheyney was lopsided with victories. Cheyney won 251 games and lost only 51 contests under head coach C. Vivian Stringer.

In 1983, Stringer moved into the Big 8 Conference (now Big 12) by accepting the head-coaching position at the University of Iowa.

At Iowa, Coach Stringer methodically continued her relentless winning ways. From 1987 to 1993, her Iowa Hawkeyes' team was ranked in the final Associated Press National Poll six times (in 1987 as number nine, in 1988 as number two, in 1989 as number eight, in 1990 as number ten, in 1992 as number seven, and in 1993 as number four).

In 1988, the Hawkeyes were twenty-nine and two, and Stringer was named the Converse National Coach of the Year. In 1993, Stringer guided the Hawkeyes through the NCAA Tournament and made her second appearance in the fabulous Final Four Championship. The championship was eventually won by Texas Tech. Ohio State finished second. Iowa and Vanderbilt rounded out the best-of-the-best list in women's basketball that season. In 1993, Stringer won Naismith, Converse, and Black Coaches Association National Coach of the Year honors.

Stringer remained at Iowa until 1995, and posted a most impressive career record of 269 wins and 84 losses.

Coach C. Vivian Stringer set down roots in the Garden State in the summer of that year. On July 14, 1995, Stringer signed a six-year contract to coach women's basketball at Rutgers, The State University of New Jersey. Coach Stringer's contract was for a base salary of $150,000 a year, with incentives and bonuses that could increase her yearly income up to $300,000. The deal made C. Vivian Stringer the highest-paid woman in college coaching at the time, and the highest-paid Rutgers coach of any sport.

The investment paid speedy dividends. In the first game Stringer coached at Rutgers (November 25, 1995), the Lady Scarlet Knights stunned women's basketball fans by upsetting seventh-ranked Penn State by a score of 69–67.

Within two years, C. Vivian Stringer had constructed a program ready to make runs at a national title. Rutgers also started to pile up twenty-win seasons.

On December 18, 1999, Rutgers topped Texas 68–64. The win was C. Vivian Stringer's six hundredth career victory. The team went on to post a 26–8 record that year and earned a berth in the NCAA Tournament's Final Four. C. Vivian Stringer became the only coach in basketball history to skipper three different schools into the Final Four..

More twenty-plus seasons materialized. In 2004, C. Vivian Stringer added two dazzling gems to her diamond-studded basketball resume. On December 8, 2004, a 68–46 victory over Princeton netted Stringer her seven hundredth career victory. In the summer of 2004, C. Vivian Stringer was named one of Coach Van Chancellor's assistants with the U.S. Women'sOlympic Basketball Squad. Another of his Olympic assistant coaches was New Jersey's Anne Donovan. The women's basketball squad won a gold medal at the 2004 Olympic Games in Athens, Greece.

The winning ways continued at Rutgers. In 2006–07, the Lady Knights recorded their fifth straight season with twenty or more wins. Rutgers clawed its way to victory after victory in the NCAA Tournament. Along the way they upset Duke, the number-one-ranked team in the country. To reach to the title game, Rutgers ripped LSU 59–35 in Final Four play.

"Wow! That's the best word to describe what's going on here," Stringer told the press after the win over LSU.

In 2007, Rutgers met the University of Tennessee, coached by Pat Summett for the National Championship. In a hard-fought contest, Tennessee emerged from the fray the victor. The loss was tough to take, but everyone concerned knew Rutgers was not a one-season wonder. The Lady Scarlet Knights, coached by C. Vivian Stringer, would be back.

On February 27, 2008, Rutgers defeated DePaul 60–46 in a Big East Conference clash. The victory was Coach Stringer's eight hundredth career win. It made her one of the most successful coaches in the history of women's basketball. After the game, Coach C. Vivian Stringer told the press, "I'm the most fortunate person in the world, because I've spent my life coaching basketball."

Coach Stringer has groomed many of her players for successful careers in sports-related fields, including professional athletics and coaching. Counted among her numerous protégés are WNBA stars Cappie Pondexter, Tammy Sutton-Brown, and Chelsea Newton. Former associates who are coaches include ex-Harlem Globetrotter Jolette Law, who coaches for Illinois; Lisa Stone, who coaches for Wisconsin; and Marianna Freeman, who coaches for Syracuse.

C. Vivian Stringer was inducted into the Women's Basketball Hall of Fame in 2001. She is also included in the Sports Hall of Fame of New Jersey, the International Women's Sports Hall of Fame, and the University of Iowa Athletics Hall of Fame.

C. Vivian Stringer– Courtesy Jim O'Connor/Rutgers Athletic Communications

C. Vivian Stringer received the Black Coaches Association's Lifetime Achievement Award in 2004

C. Vivian Stringer–Courtesy Larry Levanti/Rutgers Athletic Communications

JOSEPH R.THEISMANN
Football
South River, New Jersey
Born: September 9, 1949

Joseph "Joe" Theismann was a superb all-around athlete, who starred as a quarterback in football and as a shortstop in baseball at South River High School in New Jersey during the 1960s. Theismann was a slick-fielding, speedy-leadoff hitter on the baseball diamond, but it was on the football gridiron that he truly excelled.

In his senior season (1966) Joe Theismann led his South River football squad to a perfect 9–0 record and was voted First Team All-State by the Associated Press. Joining Theismann on that 1966 AP All-State football team were future NFL stars Franco Harris and Jack Tatum. The South River signal caller's senior stats were impressive, and peeked the interest of top college football scouts from coast to coast. Theismann completed 95 of 198 passes for 1,691 yards and twenty-three touchdowns. Joe could run with the pigskin as well as he could pass it, and personally accounted for eight rushing touchdowns.

After being courted by college football's most prestigious pigskin programs, Joe Theismann accepted a football scholarship to the University of Notre Dame.

At Notre Dame, the six foot one inch, 179-pound Theismann was nicknamed "the South River Road Runner" by sportswriters because of his ability to scramble with the football. Sophomore QB Joe Theismann got the opportunity to start for the Irish when senior signal caller Terry Hanratty suffered a knee injury midway through the 1968 season.

Notre Dame Coach Ara Parseghian once described the versatile Theismann this way in a press conferencez; "He's the type of quarterback I hate to play against," said Parseghian. "His darting quickness is a real asset." Theismann helped the Irish complete a 7–2–1 season in 1968, and guided Notre Dame to an 8–2–1 record in 1969.

It was at Notre Dame that the pronunciation of the former South River star's last name was forever altered. While in New Jersey, Joe's last name was always pronounced 'Thees-man." At Notre Dame, the pronunciation was changed to "Thighs-man." The modification was part of a Notre Dame Heisman Trophy campaign that trumped the slogan, "Theismann as in Heisman".

Joe Theismann did not win the coveted trophy that goes to the top college football player in America. Theismann finished second to quarterback Jim Plunkett of Stanford, who won the Heisman in 1970.

However, Theismann, who led the Irish to a 10–1 record, including a Cotton Bowl upset victory over Texas, was named an Academic All-American. His career stats at Notre Dame were outstanding. Joe completed 290 of 509 passes for 4,411 yards and thirty-one touchdowns. He also rushed for over one thousand yards.

Joe Theismann's size worked against him as a professional football prospect. Pro scouts thought he was too small to function as an NFL field general. Theismann was a mid-round selection of the Miami Dolphins, who planned to use Joe as a defensive back. Theismann spurned the National Football League and signed a pro contract to play quarterback for the Toronto Argonauts of the Canadian Football League. Joe Theismann played three seasons in the CFL and completed 382 of 679 passes for 6,093 yards and forty touchdowns.

In 1974, the Washington Redskins of the National Football League signed Joe Theismann to a contract. At first, Theismann acted as a backup QB, and occasionally returned punts. Joe became the Redskins' starting quarterback in 1978.

In 1982, Joe Theismann led the Washington Redskins to an NFC Championship by completing 161 of 252 passes for 2,033 yards and thirteen TDs. The Redskins went on to win Super Bowl XVII by beating the Miami Dolphins 27–7. In the game, Theismann completed fifteen of twenty-three passes for 143 yards and two touchdowns. Joe Theismann shared the NFL's Most Valuable Player Award in 1982 with placekicker Mark Moseley of Washington and Dan Fouts of the San Diego Chargers.

In 1982, the Washington Redskins, guided by QB Joe Theismann, returned to the Super Bowl, but were beaten 38–9 by the Oakland Raiders. In 1983, Theismann shared the league's Most Valuable Player Award with Redskins' running back John Riggins. Joe Theismann was also named the Associated Press NFL Player of the Year that season. In 1984, Theismann was voted the Most Valuable Player of the NFL Pro Bowl.

Quarterback Joe Theismann suffered a horrific injury in an NFL contest broadcast live on television in 1985. New York Giants' linebacker Lawrence Taylor sacked Theismann as Joe dropped back to pass, and snapped the bones in Joe's leg. The severe compound fracture ended Joe Theismann's playing career.

Over twelve NFL seasons, Theismann completed 2,044 of 3,602 passes for 25,206 yards and 160 touchdowns. Joe Theismann also rushed for 1,815 yards on 355 carries and scored seventeen TDs.

Theismann became a color commentator for NFL games broadcast on television and briefly worked on *Monday Night Football*. He is now a noted TV analyst and also does television commercials and promotions.

JEFFREY ALLEN TORBORG
Baseball
Plainfield, New Jersey
Born: November 26, 1941

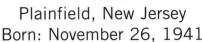

Jeff Torborg was behind the plate for the Los Angeles Dodgers on September 9, 1965, when southpaw sensation Sandy Koufax locked up in a dynamic pitching duel against hurler Bob Hendley of the Chicago Cubs. Hendley gave up only one hit that day. It was a single to Dodgers' outfielder Lou Johnson. Los Angeles also scored a lone run in the fifth inning without the benefit of a hit to cling to a slim one-to-zero advantage over Chicago.

All eyes were on the Dodgers' battery of Koufax and Torborg as super Sandy sent batter after batter back to the Cubs' dugout. In all, twenty-seven Chicago hitters, including all-time greats Ron Santo and Ernie Banks, were completely baffled by the marvelous pitching mechanics of Sandy Koufax. Meanwhile, enjoying the sights from a crouch behind the dish was former Rutgers baseball star and New Jersey native Jeff Torborg.

One by one, Koufax retired every opposing batter he faced, to record an elusive perfect game. Catcher Jeff Torborg played a part in making major-league baseball history on that day.

Jeffrey Torborg was born in Plainfield and raised in Westfield, New Jersey. After an outstanding high school sports career, Torborg enrolled at Rutgers, The State University of New Jersey. Torborg had a terrific career as a Scarlet Knights catcher from 1961 to 1963. The Rutgers baseball squad posted an incredible record of forty wins, thirteen losses, and one tie over that period. In 1963, Torborg's senior season, the talented backstop had an astounding .537 batting average. It was the highest batting average for college players with one hundred at bats or under in the nation. That same season, Jeff blasted six home runs and recorded twenty-one runs batted in. Jeff Torborg was named a First Team All-American baseball player in 1963.

Torborg's career stats in college were equally impressive. His career batting average of .390 is still one of the best ever posted at Rutgers.

Jeff Torborg was signed by the Los Angeles Dodgers as an amateur free agent in 1963 and received a $100,000 bonus. The six foot, 195-pound catcher wasted no time in getting to the big show. Torborg's major-league debut with the Dodgers was on May 10, 1964. Jeff appeared in twenty-eight games that season, sharing catching chores with John Roseboro and Doug Camilli. Torborg collected ten hits in forty-three at bats for a .233 average.

Over the years, Torborg became better known for his skills behind the plate than his ability to hit. He was a student of the game, who knew how to call pitches and how to handle hurlers. He was an expert at setting up batters for a crafty punch-out third strike.

Torborg's best two years as a hitter were in 1965, when he batted .240 (on 36 hits in 150 at bats), and in 1970, when he batted .231 (with 32 hits in 134 at bats).

As already mentioned, Jeff Torborg's real value as a major leaguer was his ability as a consummate backstop. In addition to catching Sandy Koufax's perfect game in 1965, Torborg had a hand in another Dodger no-hitter in 1970. On July 20, 1970, Los Angeles pitcher Bill Singer no-hit the Philadelphia Phillies. The Dodgers won a seven-to-zero victory on that day, and once again, Jeff Torborg was the receiver of record.

In 1971, Jeff Torborg was traded to the California Angels. Torborg remained with the Angels until 1973, the year he collected a career-best fifty-six hits in a season. On May 15, 1973, Jeff Torborg was squatting behind the dish when the Angels' Nolan Ryan fired a no-hitter against the Kansas City Royals. California won 3–0, and Nolan Ryan chalked up the first of seven no-hitters he collected over the course of his illustrious career.

The fabulous feat was also a memorable moment in the big-league career of Jeff Torborg. It was the third time he'd caught a no-hit game. At the end of the 1973 season, Torborg retired as a player.

However, Torborg's affiliation with major-league baseball was far from over. It was time for stage two of his hardball career. Torborg became a major-league coach and a big-league manager-in-waiting. Jeff's wait was over by the year 1977. Jeff Torborg was named the manager of the Cleveland Indians that season. In his first year at the helm of the Indians, he guided the Tribe to a record of forty-five wins and fifty-nine losses. He remained with Cleveland until the end of the 1979 season. In three years he skippered the Indians to 157 wins and 201 losses.

After a short absence as a major-league manager, Torborg took control of the Chicago White Sox in 1989. His first year at Chicago, he won sixty-nine games and lost ninety-two games. The following year, Torborg righted the sinking Sox ship. In 1990, the Chicago White Sox reversed their direction and won 94 of 162 games. Skipper Jeff Torborg was named the American League Manager of the Year in 1990.

Torborg followed up his banner year with another solid season. In 1991, he mentored the Sox to a record of eighty-seven wins and seventy-five losses. In 485 games as the Chicago manager, Jeff Torborg won 250 games and lost 235 games.

Torborg then jumped from the Windy City to the city that never sleeps. He returned to the East Coast and landed in the Big Apple as the manager of the New York Mets. In two hundred games as the Mets' field marshal, Torborg was victorious in only eighty-five contests. Jeff Torborg was replaced by Dallas Green in the 1993 season.

Torborg then worked as a TV broadcaster, doing major-league games until 2001. Next, he assumed the leadership of the Montreal Expos for a single season. Torborg then traded cold Canada for the Sunshine State, and worked as the manager of the Florida Marlins from 2002 to 2003.

Jeff then returned to broadcasting as a color analyst for the Atlanta Braves. The former big-league backstop remained at his post behind a microphone until 2006.

Bigleague manager Jeff Torborg skippered a total of 1,352 games. He chalked up 634 victories and suffered 718 defeats. He enjoyed a long major-league career as a player, coach, manager, and broadcaster, one that lasted from 1964 to 2003. He shared great pitching moments in baseball, catching for Hall of Famers Sandy Koufax , Don Drysdale, and Nolan Ryan.

Jeff Torborg is a member of the Rutgers Baseball Hall of Fame. He is still actively involved in the world of baseball and sports.

Jeff Torborg–Courtesy Los Angeles Dodgers

PETER KELLY TRIPUCKA
Basketball
Glen Ridge/Bloomfield, New Jersey
Born: February 16, 1959

The Tripucka clan of New Jersey is most definitely a family of outstanding athletes. Frank Tripucka, the family patriarch, got the ball rolling back in the 1940s. The Bloomfield, New Jersey, native took his athletic talents to South Bend, Indiana, to play football for the University of Notre Dame. The Fightin' Irish's gridiron squad was skippered by legendary football coach Frank Leahy.

Young Frank Tripucka was a quarterback, and a very good one at that. However, the signal-calling chores for the Irish were in the extremely capable hands of Johnny Lujack. Lujack had inherited the field-general position from Angelo Bertelli, who'd won the Heisman Trophy in 1943.

Lujack led Notre Dame to an 8–0–1 record in 1946 and a number-one ranking in the Associated Press college poll. QB Johnny Lujack guided Notre Dame to a perfect 9–0–0 record the next year (1947) and to a second straight numberone ranking. Notre Dame's Johnny Lujack won the Heisman Trophy that year.

New Jersey's Frank Tripucka backed up Lujack those two seasons, and ascended to the role of starting quarterback in 1948. Tripucka was up to the challenge, and engineered a 9–0–1 season for Notre Dame's gridiron faithful and a number-two national ranking for the Irish.

After graduating from Notre Dame, Frank Tripucka played professionally for the Denver Broncos. When his playing days were done, Frank and his wife Sandy returned to their native soil in New Jersey to raise their family.

The Tripucka family tree grew in the Garden State to include six sons and one daughter. All of the siblings were good athletes, but perhaps the best of the brood was son number five, Peter Kelly Tripucka, better known to all as Kelly.

Kelly Tripucka followed in father Frank's footsteps as a superstar in sports . . . but not on the gridiron. Kelly excelled in soccer, and especially in basketball at Bloomfield High School. Kelly was a six foot five inch forward with a great inside game. He wasn't afraid to mix it up under the rim. Tripucka tallied a total of 1,045 points his senior year in high school. Over the course of his high school career, Kelly Tripucka racked up 2,278 total points. Kelly was a New Jersey All-State performer in both basketball and soccer. He was pursued by many top college sports programs, including Duke, Maryland, and South Carolina.

True to his dad's college ties, Kelly Tripucka opted to attend the University of Notre Dame. He also decided to concentrate on a single sport in college—basketball.

Kelly Tripucka became a scoring whiz for the Irish, and led Notre Dame in scoring for four years. Three of those four years he earned All-America honors in basketball. In 1977, Notre Dame, coached by Digger Phelps, was twenty-one and six. In 1978, the Irish were twenty and six. Notre Dame posted an impressive twenty-two and five record in 1979. Kelly Tripucka led the Fightin' Irish to a twenty and seven record in 1980.

In 1981, the Detroit Pistons made Kelly Tripucka their numberone pick in the NBA player draft. He was the twelfth player selected overall. Kelly filled up the basket during his rookie season in the National Basketball Association. He scored 1,772 points as a first-year pro, and averaged 21.6 points per game. Tripucka was named to the 1981–82 NBA All-Star squad.

Kelly Tripucka played with Isiah Thomas, Kent Benson, and Phil Hubbard at Detroit. His second year, he poured in 1,536 points for a 26.5 points-per-game average and was again selected to play in the National Basketball Association's All-Star game.

Tripucka remained a Piston until the end of the 1985–86 season. Kelly was then traded to the Utah Jazz for Adrian Dantly. His two-year stay in Utah was a bad fit, and his scoring average and playing time dipped below his usual outstanding numbers. In 1988–89, he joined the Charlotte Hornets and rebounded with a vengeance. Tripucka stung NBA defenders for 1,606 total points and an average of 22.6 points per game.

Sharpshooter Kelly Tripucka closed out his NBA career as a member of the Charlotte Hornets. His last active season on the court was in 1990–91. Over the span of his ten-year pro-hoop career, Kelly Tripucka netted a total of 12,142 points. He had a career average of 17.2 points per game. Kelly also ripped down 2,703 rebounds and dished out 2,090 assists. In play-off action (twenty-five games), the New Jersey native added 391 points, ninety-three rebounds, and fifty-seven assists to his total stats.

In 2000, Kelly Tripucka was named to the National Polish-American Hall of Fame. Tripucka was inducted into the Sports Hall of Fame of New Jersey in 2005. Kelly Tripucka continues to work in basketball as a color commentator for TV broadcasts and as a professional NBA scout.

Kelly Tripucka–Courtesy University of Notre dame
Sports Information

Kelly Tripucka averaged 21.6 points per game
as a rookie player for the Detroit Pistons

JERSEY JOE WALCOTT
Boxing
Merchantville, New Jersey
Born: January 31, 1914

Arnold Raymond Cream was his real name. He was the fifth of twelve children in his family. Childhood friends called him "Reds" because he had a tuft of red hair. His father died when Reds was only thirteen years old. He had to quit school and get a job to help support his family. Arnold worked in a soap factory. He sold newspapers. Reds pushed around a wheelbarrow at construction sites. The young man was desperate to make money.

During his free time, young Arnold began to hang around Battling Mac's Gym in Camden, New Jersey, and discovered he had a knack for using his fists inside a boxing ring. And so the persona known as "Joe Walcott" was created.

The name came from a famous welterweight boxing champion born in Barbados that Arnold's father had told him about when he was a boy. Since Arnold Cream was born in Merchantville, New Jersey, he added "Jersey" to his borrowed moniker.

Arnold Cream fought his first bout as a pro before he began to use his new name. He faced a fighter named Cowboy Wallace in a small arena in Vineland, New Jersey on September 9, 1930. Arnold was only sixteen years old at the time, and he was raw in the ring. He was also a game fighter. Cream creamed Wallace, knocking him cold in round one. The victory earned Arnold a prize purse of seven dollars and fifty cents. It wasn't much, but the money helped boost the family fund, and it beat selling newspapers or pushing a wheelbarrow. From that night on, Arnold Cream was a prizefighter.

After eleven straight wins, Arnold finally assumed the ring identity of Jersey Joe Walcott. In 1933, Jersey Joe lost his first fight. The bout took place in Philadelphia, Pennsylvania, and Walcott lost on points to a fighter named Henry Wilson.

Walcott's career had highs and lows as he struggled for years to earn a living. He married and started his own family, so his need to succeed became even greater. At one point, he accepted a job as a sparring partner for boxing rival Joe Louis. At the time, Louis was training for a run at the World Heavyweight Championship. The job was short-lived for Walcott. On the first day of ring work, Joe Walcott knocked Joe Louis to the canvas. Walcott didn't realize it was his job to take punishment and not to dish it out. He was fired. Joe Louis went on to win the heavyweight crown from James J. Braddock, and Joe Walcott's ring career went into a tailspin.

Jersey Joe, who was a deeply religious man, searched his soul for an answer. At the end of 1941, Walcott quit prizefighting and took a regular job at the Camden shipyards.

In 1944, boxing matchmaker, Felix Bocchicchio, lured Jersey Joe out of retirement. Walcott was over thirty years old at the time. Jersey Joe's return to the ring was a main-event bout in New York's Madison Square Garden against Lee Oma, a seasoned and cagey fighter. Jersey Joe showed flashes of his old form and beat Oma on points. Once again, Jersey Joe took a roller-coaster ride. He lost to Tiger Jack Fox and was KO'd by heavyweight contender Abe Simon.

In 1945, Jersey Joe bested some top heavyweights, including Jimmy Bivins, Joe Baksi, and Curtis Sheppard.

In 1946 and 1947, Walcott lost a tough bout to former light heavyweight champion Joey Maxim, but avenged the defeat with a victory in a return match. Walcott was finally earning enough money as a fighter to support his family. However, the clock was ticking, and time was running out for Jersey Joe. He was past thirty, and old by ring standards.

Nevertheless, Walcott's record of forty-five wins, eleven loses, and one draw made him a top contender for the heavyweight crown. Jersey Joe got his shot against World Champion Joe Louis on December 5, 1947. The bout was the first championship fight ever seen on TV. No one gave old Jersey Joe much of a chance against the great Joe Louis. Of course, that opinion changed early in the first round of the bout when a crunching right from Walcott to the chin of Louis sent the champion to the floor. Walcott befuddled Louis with quick jabs and short hooks throughout the fight. In the fourth round, Jersey Joe Walcott once again dumped Joe Louis on the canvas. When the final bell sounded to end round fifteen, both fighters were still on their feet. The crowd roared their approval of Walcott's masterful performance. The fans thought he'd stolen the heavyweight crown from the great Joe Louis. The judges ruled otherwise. Joe Louis retained his title on a very unpopular split decision.

Three months later, on June 25, 1948, Jersey Joe Walcott and Joe Louis met in a title rematch at Yankee Stadium. Once again, Walcott got the best of the defending champion. For ten rounds, Louis remained puzzled by Walcott's technique. In round eleven, Joe Louis solved the mystery. The champion trapped

Jersey Joe in a corner and fired punch after deadly punch. Walcott crumpled to the canvas and was counted out. Joe Louis won by a knockout.

Another title shot seemed highly unlikely for the thirty-five-year-old Jersey Joe Walcott. However, fate stepped in and provided a unique opportunity for several heavyweight hopefuls. On March 1, 1949, Joe Louis, the famed Brown Bomber, retired from boxing with a record of sixty-eight wins (fifty-four KOs) and three defeats. The heavyweight crown was declared vacant and up for grabs.

The National Boxing Association determined that Jersey Joe Walcott, age thirty-five, and Ezzard Charles, age twenty-eight, should square off in the ring for a title fight. The eventual winner would wear the heavyweight crown as world champion.

The title bout was held on June 22, 1949, in Chicago's Comiskey Park. Jersey Joe Walcott, the oldest fighter ever to battle for the heavyweight title, took on younger foe Ezzard Charles. The bout was televised, but the fighters did not put on much of a show. They both seemed cautious and tentative throughout the fight. Charles won the title in a fifteen-round decision.

The defeat was a record-setting one for Jersey Joe. No boxer had ever lost three consecutive championship fights before.

Walcott added another bitter loss to that string after posting several impressive victories in 1950. He beat Swedish champion Ollie Tandberg in Stockholm. He bested Johnny Shkor, Hein Ten Hoff, and Harold Johnson. The win over young Harold Johnson was sort of a family affair. Fourteen years earlier, Jersey Joe Walcott had beaten Harold's father, Phil Johnson, in the ring.

On March 7, 1951, Jersey Joe and Ezzard Charles met in a rematch, and Walcott lost his fourth championship fight.

A short time later, fight fans were stunned when it was announced that Jersey Joe Walcott would once again take on Ezzard Charles in another title bout. It was like déjà vu all over again. The two familiar foes faced off in Pittsburgh, Pennsylvania, on July 18, 1951. Jersey Joe was thirty-seven years old at the time, but had the body, muscles, and stamina of a much younger man. He also had the heart of a lion.

It was in the seventh round of the title clash that the lion roared. A crashing left hook from Jersey Joe caught Ezzard on the chin, and he crashed to the canvas. The referee counted out the reigning champion, and a new ruler ascended to the heavyweight throne. Jersey Joe Walcott, at age thirty-seven, won the heavyweight championship of the world. After he won the championship, all Jersey Joe could say was, "Thank God! Thank God!"

Walcott remained the oldest fighter to hold a world title until 1994, when George Foreman won the heavyweight crown at age forty-five.

Walcott met Ezzard Charles one last time in a championship bout on June 5, 1952. Walcott retained his title with a fifteen-round decision.

Rocky Marciano beat Joe Walcott on September 22, 1952, and became champion. On May 15, 1953, Jersey Joe took one last stab at the title. Marciano knocked out Walcott in round one to demolish that dream.

After more than twenty-two years in the ring, Jersey Joe Walcott found new fame after boxing. He appeared in a Hollywood movie with Humphrey Bogart. He refereed the World Heavyweight Championship fight between Sonny Liston and Muhammad Ali. In 1972, he was elected sheriff of Camden County in New Jersey. Joe Walcott served on the New Jersey State Athletic Commission from 1975 to 1984.

Arnold Raymond Cream, aka Jersey Joe Walcott,. He was inducted into the International Boxing Hall of Fame in 1990. He passed away on February 25, 1994, at eighty years of age

DAVID BRUCE WOHL
Basketball
East Brunswick, New Jersey
Born: November 2, 1949

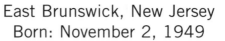

When the Los Angeles Lakers, led by Kareem Abdul-Jabbar and Magic Johnson, bested the Boston Celtics, led by Larry Bird, in the 1985 NBA Championship Series, Dave Wohl was there. He was an assistant coach to Lakers' head coach Pat Riley. When the University of Pennsylvania won two Ivy League titles and posted a two-season record of fifty-three and three (1970 and 1971), David Wohl was there. He was a star guard on the Quakers' club. When East Brunswick High School was a powerhouse program in New Jersey high school sports, Dave Wohl was there. He was a gifted all-around athlete.

Dave Wohl was born in Flushing, New York, but played high school sports in East Brunswick, New Jersey. Wohl was a talented athlete who excelled in basketball and football, earning berths on numerous all-star teams in both sports. Wohl was recruited to play football at the University of Pennsylvania. In the past, the Quakers' gridiron program had produced Philadelphia Eagles' stars Chuck Bednarik and Frank Reagan. Dave Wohl jumped at the chance. At the University of Pennsylvania, he would get an Ivy League education and could also play basketball.

Wohl did well in the classroom at Penn, but found himself to be more comfortable on a college basketball court than on a football gridiron. Dave Wohl paired with Steve Bilsky to give the Quakers one of the bestback court hoop combos in the nation. (Bilsky later went on to become the athletic director of Penn.) In 1970, the Penn Quakers posted an overall record of twenty-five and two and were ranked as high as number thirteen in the country. The following year, Penn finished the regular season undefeated at twenty-six and zero and were ranked as the number-three team in the nation. The Quakers went to the Eastern Finals in the NCAA Regional and finished the year with a record of twenty-eight wins and one loss.

Dave Wohl completed his Ivy League court education with a total of 823 points and 345 assists. He was twice named to the All-Ivy League Basketball Team. After graduating from the University of Pennsylvania, he signed with the Philadelphia 76ers. Wohl was selected by Philadelphia in the third round of the 1971 National Basketball Association draft. The six foot two inch,185-pound guard was the forty-sixth player picked in the draft overall.

Dave Wohl had a solid rookie season for the 76ers in 1971–72. He proved to be an intelligent player and a keen student of the game. Dave was also a capable ball handler, a precise passer, and a reliable defender. Wohl tallied a total of 642 points and dished out 228 assists in his initial NBA season.

The next year, however, David Wohl moved on to the Portland Trailblazers, where he played with NBA stars Geoff Petrie and Sidney Wicks. Later in the season, Dave Wohl bounced over to the new Buffalo Braves club (now the Los Angeles Clippers). In Buffalo, Wohl was soon joined by another ex-Ivy League star, Ernie DiGregorio of Providence. Also on hand was Bob McAdoo, who would win NBA scoring titles in 1974, 1975, and 1976. Before the 1973–74 season concluded, Dave Wohl packed his bags and joined the Houston Rockets. Wohl became a well-traveled pro nomad for a time, but Dave soaked up key aspects of the game of pro basketball along the way. What he learned would serve him well in his later careers as an NBA scout, coach, and general manager. Dave's final stop as a player was in his own backyard. He finished his playing career as a member of the New York-New Jersey Nets. Dave Wohl spent seven years as a pro player in the NBA and played in over four hundred games. He tallied a total of 2,553 points and collected 1,397 assists. He also added 219 steals and 558 rebounds.

When one door closed for Dave Wohl in the NBA, another opened. Wohl began a long and successful coaching career in the National Basketball Association. After serving a stint as an assistant coach with the NBA-champion Los Angeles Lakers in 1985, Dave Wohl was named the head coach of the New Jersey Nets. Wohl skippered the Nets from 1985 to 1987 and steered his club into an NBA play-off appearance in 1986.

Once again, Dave Wohl danced to the tune of a little traveling music on the winding NBA road. Along the way, he continued to add impressive accomplishments to his pro-court resume. He served as a scout and an assistant coach for the Miami Heat. Dave worked on television as an analyst for NBA broadcasts. He served assistant coaching tours with the Sacramento Kings and the Los Angeles Clippers.

From 1995 to 1997, Dave Wohl was executive vice president of basketball operations for the Miami Heat. Wohl added assistant coaching stays with the Lakers and the Orlando Magic, where he worked with head coach Glen "Doc" Rivers. When Doc Rivers became the head coach of the Boston Celtics in 2004–05, Wohl went along, too.

In 2007–08, Dave Wohl served as the Celtics' assistant general manager, working with general manager and executive director of basketball operations, Danny Ainge. Ainge starred at Brigham Young University (1977–81) and played both pro baseball (Toronto Blue Jays) and pro basketball (Boston Celtics).

It appears that East Brunswick's Dave Wohl may finally settle in Boston, as the Celtics experienced a banner year in 2007–08. The Celtics won the Eastern Conference crown with a regular-season record of sixty-six wins and sixteen losses.

In all, Dave Wohl has accumulated over thirty years of experience in the NBA as a player, scout, coach, and executive. It has been a long journey, and success has followed Wohl almost every step of the way.

Dave Wohl is a member of the University of Pennsylvania Hall of Fame.

ALEXANDER F. WOJCIECHOWICZ
Football
South River, New Jersey
Born: August 12, 1915

Alexander "Alex" Wojciechowicz was the first of several South River natives who went on to earn lasting fame as professional football players. Wojciechowicz was an offensive center and defensive end who won All-State football honors at South River High School in the early 1930s. Alex was big, strong, and extremely agile. He continued his outstanding gridiron career by playing college football for Fordham University in New York.

At the time, Fordham was considered a national gridiron power. The football team was mentored by head coach Jim Crowley. Crowley was a former Notre Dame All-American who had been a member of coach Knute Rockne's famous Four Horsemen backfield.

Wojciechowicz played center and defensive line on a 1936 Fordham squad that went 5–1–2 and finished the season ranked number fifteen in the country. Starting at guard beside Wojciechowicz on that 1936 Fordham squad was a young athlete named Vince Lombardi.   Lombardi later became immortal as a renowned head coach in the National Football League.

Alex Wojciechowicz and Vince Lombardi, along with their five other line mates, were dubbed Fordham's "Seven Blocks of Granite" by the press due to their steadfast brand of play. They were seemingly unmovable blockers on offense and rigid obstacles on defense. Fordham's Seven Blocks of Granite gave up only ninety points in twenty-five games over a span of three seasons.

Wjociechowicz was one of Fordham's standout performers. He was a multi-talented athlete, who was extremely quick for a big man. In a close contest against the University of Georgia in 1936, Alex helped cement a Fordham victory by taking a lateral and racing forty-five yards for a touchdown.

In 1937, the Fordham Rams football team posted an impressive season record of seven wins, no losses, and one tie. The Rams ended the season ranked number three in the country. Alex Wojciechowicz was rewarded for his personal contributions on the gridiron by being named an All-American in 1936 and 1937.

In 1938, the Detroit Lions made Fordham's Alex Wojciechowicz their number-one pick in the NFL draft. Alex was the sixth player selected overall. Wojciechowicz was slated to play center on the offense and linebacker on defense by Detroit's head coach Gus Dorias.

Dorias, like Fordham coach Jim Crowley, was another notable Notre Dame gridiron grad. Quarterback Gus Dorias had helped popularize the use of the forward pass. Gus Dorias and end Knute Rockne had combined to form college football's first dynamic passing duo.

Many of Alex Wojciechowicz's teammates on the 1938 Detroit Lions were also destined for football immortality. Some of the gridiron icons to be included were quarterback Earl "Dutch" Clark, running back Byron "Whizzer" White, and end Bob Layden.

However, football's future greats did not mesh as a Lions unit, and Detroit never managed to win a single championship during Wojciechowicz's eight-year stay in the Motor City. On a personal level, Alex Wojciechowicz did make his mark in the league. Wojciechowicz played inspired football, and was named All-Pro in 1939 and in 1944. In 1944, Alex Wojciechowicz intercepted seven passes on defense to establish a Lions' single-season record that stood for many years.

In the middle of the 1946 season, Wojciechowicz was released by the Detroit Lions and signed by the Philadelphia Eagles. The head coach of the Eagles was Earle "Greasy" Neale, another famous football figure. Counted among Philadelphia's top players were quarterback Allie Sherman (who later became the head coach of the New York Giants) and super running back Steve Van Buren.

The Eagles were a team on a gridiron mission, and for the first time in his pro career, Alex Wojciechowicz savored the sweet taste of championship football. In 1947, the Philadelphia Eagles won the Eastern Division of the NFL and took on the Chicago Cardinals in the title contest. The Eagles' hopes of a NFL crown flew out the window as the Cardinals captured the title with a slim 28–21 victory. Philadelphia repeated as the Eastern Division winner in 1948, and once again faced off against the Chicago Cardinals for the championship. The Eagles avenged their earlier loss and bested the Cardinals seven to zero to become NFL champions.

In 1949, Alex Wojciechowicz and the Eagles competed for the NFL crown for a third straight year. This time, their opponents were the Los Angeles Rams. Philadelphia shut out Los Angeles 14–0 to secure their second straight championship.

Alex Wojciechowicz decided to end his professional football career after the 1950 season. Wojciechowicz played in 134 NFL games and had nineteen career interceptions. He was voted a member of the NFL's 1940s All-Decade Team and is listed on the Philadelphia Eagles' Honor Roll. Alex Wojciechowicz is a member of the College Football Hall of Fame and in 1963 was elected to the Pro Football Hall of Fame.

Alex Wojciechowicz died July 13, 1992, at age seventy-six.

Alex Wojciechowicz–Courtesy Detroit Lions Football

Alex Wojciechowicz played linebacker on defense and had a total of 16 interceptions during his NFL career

Alex Wojciechowicz–Courtesy Fordham University Sports Information

ERIC ORLANDO YOUNG
Baseball (Football)
New Brunswick, New Jersey
Born: May 18, 1967

Eric Young was a two-sport star for the Rutgers Scarlet Knights during his college playing days in New Jersey. After graduating from high school, Young decided not to go away to college. He was born in New Brunswick, New Jersey, the city where the main campus of Rutgers University is located.

Young had an instant impact on both the Rutgers football and baseball programs in the late 1980s. In football, he was a wide receiver and a speedy kick-return specialist. The fleet-footed Young won All-East mentions in football in 1987 and 1988. In his senior year (1988), Eric snared forty-eight passes for 592 yards and three touchdowns. Over his four-year college-football career, Young grabbed a total of 109 passes for 1,380 yards and nine touchdowns.

Eric also excelled as a kick-return specialist. He had sixty-four returns for a total of 1,451 yards on the college gridiron. Eric Young accounted for 2,928 all-purpose yards in his career.

On the baseball diamond, Eric Young sparkled as a swift and sure-handed second baseman. Twice, he was named to the Atlantic 10 All-Conference Team (in the days before Rutgers joined the Big East Conference). Young batted over .300 in his three varsity seasons, and hit .337 as a senior. His impressive career stats included 17 triples, 64 stolen bases, and 150 runs scored.

Eric Young was selected by the Los Angeles Dodgers in the 1989 player draft. After sharpening his diamond skills for a short time in the minor leagues, he joined the Dodgers in 1992, and appeared in forty-nine games, mainly as a second baseman. Young collected thirty-four hits in 132 at bats for a .258 batting average in his first taste of big-league life. He also had a double, a homer, and stole six bases.

In 1993, the Colorado Rockies entered the National League as an expansion club, and Eric Young became one of the Rockies' original team members. In fact, Young delighted Colorado fans by clubbing a home run in the Rockies' first-ever home at bat. The popularity of the ex-Rutgers star blazed brighter and brighter during his years in Colorado. His first year on the Rockies, Young batted .269 and stole forty-two bases. In 1994, the slick-fielding second baseman's average rose to .272, but his stolen base output dipped to a mere eighteen swipes. However, Eric did blast eight home runs. Young had one of his best years in the big leagues in 1995, and helped Colorado to its first appearance in postseason play. Eric Young lifted his batting average to .317 by collecting 116 hits in 366 at bats. He also stole thirty-five bases and drove in thirty-six runs.

However, Eric Young's banner year as a big leaguer was in 1996. Young sizzled in the batter's box and on the base paths. He swung a hot bat and cracked 184 hits in 568 at bats for a career-best .324 average. In addition to his solid hitting, Eric burned up the base paths by stealing fifty-three bases to lead the National League in that category. Young also clouted eight home runs and collected a total of seventy-one runs batted in. Eric Young was named the National League All-Star at second base as a reward for his spectacular output in 1996.

In 1997, Young started to see action in the outfield, in addition to his work at second base. Eric split the 1997 season with two teams. He played the beginning of the year with the Colorado Rockies and was then traded back to the Los Angeles Dodgers. The change of scenery had little if any effect on his on-field output. He smashed 174 hits in 622 at bats to post a .280 batting average. His eight home runs, eight triples, and thirty-three doubles were also impressive stats. In addition, Young pilfered forty-five bases and batted home sixty-one runs.

Eric Young continued to be amazingly consistent wherever he played during his fifteen-year baseball career. Eric Young remained a Dodger from 1997 up to 1999. In 2000, Los Angeles traded Young to the Chicago Cubs. The Windy City weather proved to be a breath of fresh air for the New Brunswick, New Jersey, native. Young upped his batting average to .297 and stole a career-best fifty-four bases. Florida's Luis Castillo won the NL stolen base crown that season with sixty-two swipes.

The Cubs and Eric Young parted company after the 2001 season. Young moved on to spend a season with the Milwaukee Brewers. As usual, Eric Young had a solid year.

In 2003, Young found himself playing Major League Baseball for the San Francisco Giants. As a Giant, Eric Young discovered a new source of power in his swing. He pounded out a career-best fifteen home runs.

At the end of the year, Young was once again on the move. He spent 2004 with the Texas Rangers and 2005 with the San Diego Padres. Then, in 2006, it was back to the Rangers.

In fifteen years in the major leagues, Eric Young banged out 1,731 hits in 6,119 at bats for a .283 career average. The speedster stole a total of 465 bases and smashed seventy-nine home runs. He also had a total of 543 runs batted in.

Eric Young's son, Eric Young Jr., who was born in Piscataway, New Jersey, now plays minor-league baseball in the Colorado Rockies' organization.

Eric Young Sr. is a member of the Rutgers Football Hall of Fame and the Rutgers Baseball Hall of Fame.

Eric Young–Courtesy Los Angeles Dodgers

ELAINE ZAYAK
Figure Skating
Paramus, New Jersey
Born: April 4, 1965

Grace. Athleticism. Balance. Rhythm. Beauty. Those are just a few of the attributes one needs to excel at the demanding sport of figure skating. Perfection is always the goal, but attainment of the ultimate score is an elusive if not impossible prize. One minor mishap or infraction, and perfection slips through the performer's grasp. A single fall and a skater's hopes for victory usually come crashing down.

Elaine Zayak dared to risk failure at the 1982 World Figure Skating Championships by attempting a myriad of exciting triple jumps. Zayak stunned the judges and astonished the crowd by landing a total of six dangerous triple jumps. It was a crowning achievement that won young Elaine Zayak a world title.

New Jersey native Elaine Zayak was born in Paramus and attended Paramus High School. Elaine lost part of her left foot in a lawn-mower accident and began to figure skate as a form of physical therapy. It soon became evident that young Miss Zayak was endowed with natural athleticism on ice that could propel her to national prominence in the sport of figure skating. Elaine was a tireless worker and a fierce competitor. She trained extremely hard, and her dedication, combined with her athletic ability, reaped whirlwind results.

In 1979, young skating sensation Elaine Zayak was crowned figure skating's Junior National Champion. The following year, Elaine was one of a group of U.S. skaters who made an historic trip to China. Before then, American skaters had never traveled to China to perform exhibitions.

Elaine Zayak made a bold leap into the glamorous realm of high-profile figure skating competitions in 1981. Zayak captured the United States National Championship, beating Priscilla Hill. At the 1981 World Figure Skating Championships, Zayak finished second to Denise Biellmann of Switzerland, who took the gold. Elaine Zayak's silver-medal performance was very impressive. She was only fifteen years old at the time.

In 1982, New Jersey teenager Elaine Zayak achieved immortal skating status at the World Championships in Copenhagen. She landed six triple jumps during a spellbinding free-skating exhibition to edge East Germany's Katarina Witt for the title. Shortly after Elaine's World Championship performance, the international governing body for figure skating created what has become known as "the Zayak Rule"

The rule was adopted to limit female competitors to only three triple jumps in a performance. The rule's purpose was to encourage skaters to display a greater variety of skills. Some skating fans claim that international judges were simply overwhelmed by the unbelievable athletic ability displayed by Elaine Zayak at the 1982 World Championships.

In 1983, an injury curtailed Elaine's meteoric rise to stardom. At the world competition in Helsinki, she suffered a stress fracture in her right ankle and was forced to withdraw. Rosalynn Sumners of the U.S. skated to the gold in 1983. Sumners also captured the U.S. Championship that same year. Elaine Zayak was the runner-up.

Unfortunately, Elaine never regained the top form she displayed in 1981 and 1982. Zayak finished third at both the U.S. Championship and the World Championship in 1984. She finished a disappointing sixth at the 1984 Olympics.

Elaine turned pro late in 1984 and signed to skate for the Ice Capades. In a surprise move, Elaine Zayak had her amateur status reinstated in 1994 in an attempt to make the U.S. Olympic Team. It was the first time such a request had ever been granted to a U.S. female figure skater. Zayak placed fourth at the U.S. Championship and was named an alternate to the U.S. Olympic quad. Her performance at the U.S. Championship included several extremely difficult triple jumps not seen on the ice in women's competition for nearly a decade.

In 2003, Elaine Zayak was inducted into the U.S. Figure Skating Hall of Fame. The following year, she was named to the Sports Hall of Fame of New Jersey.

GARDEN STATE HONOR ROLL

GARDEN STATE HONOR ROLL
One Hundred Other Notable New Jersey Sports Figures

VAL ACKERMAN

Sports Business   Pennington, New Jersey

Val Ackerman is the founding president of the Women's National Basketball Association (WNBA).

MATEE AJAVON

Basketball   Newark, New Jersey

Matee Ajavon starred for the Rutgers University women's basketball team that played for the National Championship in 2007. She was the fifth player taken in the 2008 WNBA draft and was selected by the Houston Comets.

BILLY ARD

Football   Watchung/Warren Hills, New Jersey

Bill Ard was an offensive lineman in the NFL for the New York Giants and the Green Bay Packers.

JULIETTE ATKINSON

Tennis   Rahway, New Jersey

Juliette Atkinson was the first woman player to come to the net and volley. She was the U.S. Doubles Champion with Helen Hellwig in 1894. Atkinson won singles titles in 1895, 1897, and 1898. She is included in the International Tennis Hall of Fame.

AL ATTLES

Basketball   Newark, New Jersey

Al Attles had a great NBA playing career with the Philadelphia and Golden State Warriors. Attles coached in the NBA for fourteen years and guided the Warriors to an NBA Championship in 1974–75.

THOMAS "BABE" BARLOW

Basketball   Trenton, New Jersey

Babe Barlow played for the Philadelphia Warriors from 1921 to 1927. He is a member of the Basketball Hall of Fame.

RAY BATEMAN SR.

Sports Business   Branchburg, New Jersey

Ray Bateman is a former chairman of the New Jersey Sports and Exposition Authority.

JAY BELLAMY

Football   Matawan, New Jersey

Jay Bellamy starred at Rutgers University as a defensive back and spent fourteen years in the NFL with the Seattle Seahawks and the New Orleans Saints.

BRAD BENSON

Football   Hillsborough, New Jersey

Brad Benson was an All-Pro offensive lineman with the New York Giants. He was a member of the Giants team that won a Super Bowl in 1986.

JASON BERGMAN

Baseball   Neptune/Manalapn/Forked River, New Jersey

Jason Bergman starred in baseball at Rutgers, The State University of New Jersey and went on to pitch for the Washington Nationals in the National League.

DALE BERRA

Baseball   Ridgewood, New Jersey

Dale Berra played Major League Baseball for the Pittsburgh Pirates and the Houston Astros. He is the son of baseball Hall of Famer Yogi Berra.

CHARLIE BERRY

Football/Baseball   Phillipsburg, New Jersey

Charlie Berry played both pro football and major-league baseball in the 1920s and 1930s. Berry also worked as an NFL official and an American League umpire.

ANGELO BERTELLI

Football   Clifton, New Jersey

In 1943, Angelo Bertelli was an All-American back at the University of Notre Dame and captured the Heisman Trophy that same season. Bertelli is a member of the College Football Hall of Fame.

SCOTT "BAM BAM" BIGELOW

Pro Wrestling   Neptune, New Jersey

Heavyweight Scott Bigelow was a professional wrestler and sports entertainer who grappled with Hulk Hogan, Andre the Giant, and football star Lawrence "LT" Taylor of the New York Giants.

CRAIG BIGGIO

Baseball   South Orange, New Jersey

Craig Biggio starred at Seton Hall University before he embarked upon a long and successful major-league career with the Houston Astros. Biggio smashed over three thousand hits as a Major Leaguer.

JIM BOUTON

Baseball   Newark, New Jersey

New Jersey native Jim Bouton pitched for the New York Yankees, the Houston Astros, and the Atlanta Braves. Bouton was on the 1963 American League All-Star team as a Yankee hurler.

DON "TARZAN" BRAGG

Track and Field   Penns Grove, New Jersey

Don Bragg won the NCAA Pole Vault Championship in 1955 as a student at Villanova University. Bragg won a gold medal in the pole vault event at the 1960 Olympic Games. He was famous for celebrating successful vaults by pounding his chest and yelling like Tarzan.

LESLEY BUSH

Diving   Orange, New Jersey

Lesley Bush won a gold medal at the 1964 Olympic Games in Tokyo when she wa a sixteen-year-old high school student. Bush was the National Platform Diving Champion in 1965 and 1967.

DICK BUTTON

Figure Skating   Englewood, New Jersey

Dick Button is New Jersey's greatest male figure skater. He won two Olympic gold medals and was a five-time World Champion. Button worked as a TV sportscaster, covering the sport of figure skating for many years.

BEN CARNEVALE

Basketball   Raritan, New Jersey

After serving as the captain of the NYU basketball team in 1937–38, Ben Carnevale had a brief pro-basketball career. Carnevale later coached at the University of North Carolina and the United States Naval Academy. He is a member of the Basketball Hall of Fame.

RYAN CARSEY

Track   Hunterdon County, New Jersey

Ryan Carsey is a legally blind distance runner.

ESSENCE CARSON

Basketball   Paterson, New Jersey

Essence Carson was a starter on the Rutgers women's basketball squad that finished second to Tennessee in the 2007 NCAA Tournament. Carson was picked by the New York Liberty in the first round of the WNBA draft in 2008.

GEORGE CASE

Baseball   Trenton, New Jersey

George Case played for the Washington Senators and led the American League with fifty-one stolen bases in 1939. Case topped the AL in steals six times in eleven major-league seasons. He collected 1,415 hits for a lifetime batting average of .282.

SEAN CASEY

Baseball   Willingboro, New Jersey

Sean Casey has played major-league baseball for the Cleveland Indians, the Cincinnati Reds, the Pittsburgh Pirates, and the Boston Red Sox. He hit .332 and blasted twenty-five home runs in 1999 as a member of the Cincinnati Reds.

FRANK CHAPOT

Equestrian   Neshanic Station, New Jersey

Frank Chapot is a two-time Olympic silver-medal winner. He has coached numerous medal-winning equestrian teams and is a member of the Show Jumping Hall of Fame.

WAYNE CHREBET

Football   Garfield, New Jersey

Wide receiver Wayne Chrebet starred at Hofstra and played in the National Football League from 1995 to 2005. Chrebet caught 580 passes for 7,365 yards as a member of the New York Jets.

BOB CLOTWORTHY

Diving   Newark, New Jersey

Bob Clotworthy earned a gold medal in the springboard diving event at the 1956 Olympic Games. He was an NCAA Springboard Diving Champion in 1952 while at Ohio State University. Clotworthy is a member of the International Swimming Hall of Fame.

TOM COURTNEY

Track and Field   Newark, New Jersey

Tom Courtney captured a gold medal in the 800-meter run at the 1956 Olympic Games. He won the AAU 880-Yard Championship in 1957 and 1958. Courtney is included in the National Track and Field Hall of Fame.

DOC CRAMER

Baseball   Beach Haven, New Jersey

Doc Cramer topped the American League with two hundred hits in 1940 while a member of the Boston Red Sox. Cramer was named a Major League All-Star five times during his career.

LOU CREEKMUR

Football   Hope Lawn, New Jersey

Tackle/guard Lou Creekmur was an All-NFL player six times. Creekmur is a member of the Pro Football Hall of Fame.

FRANK CUMINSKY

Gymnastics   West New York, New Jersey

Frank Cuminsky won five all-around National Championships in gymnastics and twenty-two total national gymnastics titles. He was also a member of the 1948 U.S. Olympic team.

JACK CUST

Baseball   Hunterdon County, New Jersey

Jack Cust was an All-State baseball player in New Jersey at Immaculata High School in Somerville. He played major-league baseball with several clubs, including San Diego Padres.

STANLEY DANCER

Harness Racing   Edinburg, New Jersey

Stanley Dancer was harness racing's top money winner in 1961, 1962, 1964, and 1966. He was named the Harness Driver of the Year in 1968.

MARY DECKER

Track   Flemington, New Jersey

Distance runner Mary Decker was named the Associated Press Female Athlete of the Year in 1982 for setting world records in the mile, 2,000-meter, and 3,000-meter races. Decker also won the Sullivan Award as America's top amateur athlete that same year.

PETER DEPAOLO

Auto Racing   Roseland, New Jersey

Peter DePaolo won the Indy 500 in 1925, becoming the first driver to exceed the 100 mph barrier. (He averaged 101.13 mph.) He is included in the Indianapolis Speedway Hall of Fame.

JOSEPH DEPIETRO

Weight Lifting   Paterson, New Jersey

Joseph DePietro won a gold medal in weight lifting's bantamweight division at the 1948 Olympic Games. DePietro won nine U.S. Weight Lifting Championships.

MARK DEROSA

Baseball   Passaic, New Jersey

Mark DeRosa starred on the diamond at New Jersey's Bergen Catholic High School. DeRosa has played in the major leagues with the Texas Rangers, the Chicago Cubs, and the Atlanta Braves. He has over 450 career hits.

JOETTA CLARK DIGGS

Track   East Orange/Neshanic, New Jersey

Joetta Clark Diggs was a four-time Olympian who won a gold medal at the Pan American Games in 1980.

MAE FAGGS

Track   Mays Landing, New Jersey

Mae Faggs won twelve National Sprint Championships, including the 100-yard dash in 1955 and 1956. She earned an Olympic gold medal in 1952 as a member of the U.S. 4 x 100 Relay Team.

CASEY FOSSUM

Baseball   Cherry Hill, New Jersey

Casey Fossum has pitched for the Boston Red Sox, the Arizona Diamondbacks, the Tampa Bay Rays, and the Pittsburgh Pirates. He was the third player picked in the first round of the 1999 baseball draft.

IRVING FRYER

Football   Mount Holly, New Jersey

Irving Fryer was an All-American receiver at the University of Nebraska. He caught 851 passes for 12,785 yards and eighty-four touchdowns as a wide receiver in the NFL.

RICH GLOVER

Football   Bayonne, New Jersey

Rich Glover was an All-American defensive lineman at the University of Nebraska. In 1972, he won the Outland Award as America's outstanding college lineman.

EUGENE GRABOWSKI

Soccer   Newark, New Jersey

Eugene Grabowski was an All-American and Olympic soccer player.

ROSEY GRIER

Football   Roselle, New Jersey

Rosey Grier was an All-American tackle at Penn State University. He starred for the New York Giants and the Los Angeles Rams in the NFL. Grier also had a successful TV acting career.

MARVIN HAGLER

Boxing   Newark, New Jersey

Marvelous Marvin Hagler was a champion middleweight boxer who was inducted into the International Boxing Hall of Fame in 1993.

BILLY HAMILTON

Baseball   Newark, New Jersey

In 1890, Billy Hamilton stole 102 bases as a member of the Philadelphia Phillies. In fourteen major-league seasons, he posted a .344 career batting average and collected 2,158 hits. He stole a total of 912 bases. Hamilton is a member of the Baseball Hall of Fame.

JEFF HAMMONDS

Baseball   Scotch Plains, New Jersey

Speedster Jeff Hammonds played in the major leagues for the Baltimore Orioles, the Cincinnati Reds, and the Milwaukee Brewers.

FRED HILL

Baseball   Verona, New Jersey

In over forty years as a head baseball coach at Rutgers University and Montclair State University, Fred Hill has won over 950 games. Hill was a three- sport star at Upsala College in New Jersey. His oldest son, Fred Jr., is the head coach of the men's basketball team at Rutgers University.

JOHN HILL

Football   Somerset, New Jersey

John Hill was a Little All-American in football at Lehigh University. He played in the East-West College Football All-Star Game and starred in the NFL as an offensive lineman for the New York Giants and the New Orleans Saints.

John Hill is a member of the New Orleans Saints Hall of Fame

John Hill–Courtesy Lehigh University Athletics

TIM HOWARD

Soccer   North Brunswick, New Jersey

Tim Howard is a U.S. Soccer Team goalie and pro soccer player.

BOB HURLEY

Basketball   Jersey City, New Jersey

Coach Bob Hurley has made St. Anthony's High School in New Jersey a legendary national power. He has prepped many players for basketball careers at Division 1 college programs and eventually the NBA.

DWAYNE JARRETT

Football   New Brunswick, New Jersey

Dwayne Jarrett was an All-American wide receiver at the University of Southern California. He was the second-round pick of the Carolina Panthers in the 2007 NFL draft.

ASJHA JONES

Basketball   Piscataway, New Jersey

Asjha Jones was a member of the University of Connecticut's women's basketball team that won NCAA titles in 2000 and 2002. Jones played in 138 games for the Huskies and earned All-America honors. She was selected in the first round of the 2002 WNBA draft by the Washington Mystics and was the fourth player picked overall.

NATE JONES

Fooball   Scotch Plains/Fanwood, New Jersey

Nate Jones was the Big East Special Teams Player of the Year while at Rutgers. Jones has excelled as a safety in the NFL for the Dallas Cowboys since 2002.

ERIC KARROS

Baseball   Hackensack, New Jersey

Eric Karros is a star first baseman who was the 1992 National League Rookie of the Year for the Los Angeles Dodgers. Karros has played for other major-league clubs, including the Chicago Cubs.

DANNY KASS

Snow Sports   Vernon, New Jersey

Danny Kass is a world-famous professional snowboarder.

WILLIAM KNECHT

Rowing   Camden, New Jersey

William Knecht won a gold medal at the 1964 Olympics. He was part of the champion U.S. Crew Team in the eight-oared shell event. Knecht also won three gold medals in the Pan American Games.

BILL LARNED

Tennis   Summit, New Jersey

Bill Larned won the NCAA Singles Championship in 1892 while he was a student at Cornell. Larned won seven national singles titles between 1901 and 1911. He also served with Teddy Roosevelt's Rough Riders during the Spanish-American War. He is a member of the International Tennis Hall of Fame.

GUS LESNEVICH

Boxing   Cliffside Park, New Jersey

Gus Lesnevich was the light heavyweight boxing champion of the world in 1941.

MARTY LIQUORI

Track   Cedar Grove, New Jersey

Marty Liquori was the third American high school runner to break the four-minute mile (1967). He was a star distance runner at Villanova University.

RAY LUCAS

Football   Jackson, New Jersey

Ray Lucas was a star quarterback at Rutgers University. In the NFL, he played for the New York Jets and the New England Patriots. He now works as a TV analyst of NFL games.

SPARKY LYLE

Baseball   Bridgewater, New Jersey

Sparky Lyle won the American League's Cy Young Award in 1977 while pitching for the New York Yankees. He has been the manager of the highly successful minor-league Somerset Patriots in New Jersey since 1998.

SHAWN MAYER

Football   Hillsborough, New Jersey

Defensive safety Shawn Mayer starred at Penn State University and was a member of the New England Patriots team that won the Super Bowl in 2004.

LINUS MCATEE

Horse Racing   Frenchtown, New Jersey

Jockey Linus McAtee rode Whiskey to victory in the 1927 Kentucky Derby and Clyde Van Dusen to a win in the 1929 Kentucky Derby. McAtee was the nation's top money winner in 1928 and is a member of the National Horse Racing Hall of Fame.

GEORGE MEHNERT

Wrestling   Newark, New Jersey

Grappler George Mehnert won an Olympic gold medal as a flyweight in 1904 and an Olympic gold medal as a bantamweight in 1908.

DEBBIE MEYER

Swimming   Haddonfield, New Jersey

Debbie Meyer won three gold medals in freestyle swimming at the 1968 Olympic Games.

LYDELL MITCHELL

Football   Salem, New Jersey

Lydell Mitchell was an All-America halfback at Penn State. Mitchell scored twenty-nine touchdowns in 1971. He later starred in the NFL for the Baltimore Colts.

ERIC MURDOCK

Basketball   Bridgewater/Raritan, New Jersey

Guard Eric Murdock starred at Providence College in the Big East Conference and was noted for his stellar defensive skills. He played in the NBA for the Milwaukee Bucks.

RENALDO NEHEMIAH

Track   Newark, New Jersey

Renaldo Nehemiah was a world-class high hurdler from 1979 to 1989. Nehemiah was the first man to run the high hurdles in under thirteen seconds. He also tried out in the NFL with the Pittsburgh Steelers.

DON NEWCOMBE

Baseball   Madison, New Jersey

Pitcher Don Newcombe began his pro-baseball career with the Newark Eagles in the Negro league. Newcombe went on to star for the Brooklyn and Los Angeles Dodgers. His first major-league season was in 1949, when he won seventeen games. In 1956, Don Newcombe won the Cy Young Award for posting a fantastic mound record of twenty-seven wins and seven losses.

MARSHALL NEWELL

Football   Clifton, New Jersey

Marshall Newell was a four-time All-American tackle at Harvard (1890–93). He was Cornell's first football coach and is included in the College Football Hall of Fame.

ORLANDO PALMEIRO

Baseball   Hoboken, New Jersey

Outfielder Orlando Palmeiro played in the major leagues for the Anaheim Angels and the Saint Louis Cardinals.

BILL RAFTERY

Basketball   Kearny, New Jersey

Bill Raftery scored 2,192 points as a high school player at St. Cecilia's High School in New Jersey. Raftery played at LaSalle University and was drafted by the New York Knicks, but never made it in the NBA. He coached at Fairleigh Dickinson University and at Seton Hall, where he posted a 154–141 record as the Pirates' head basketball coach. He now works as a TV broadcaster of college basketball games.

Bill Raftery–Courtesy S.R. Smith/Seton Hall University

Bill Rafferty has worked as a basketball analyst for ESPN.

Bill Rafferty was a high school sports legend in New Jersey and was All-State in basketball, soccer and baseball.

Bill Raftery–Courtesy S.R.Smith/Seton Hall University

CLAUDIO REYNA

Soccer   Springfield, New Jersey

Claudio Reyna was a three-time college All-American in soccer and played on the U.S. soccer squad in 1992 and 1996.

PHIL RIZZUTO

Baseball   Hillside, New Jersey

Shortstop Phil Rizzuto was nicknamed "the Scooter" and is a Hall of Fame infielder who played for the fabled New York Yankees. Rizzuto was a five-time All-Star and was voted the Most Valuable Player in the American League in 1950. He collected 1,588 hits over his career and is a member of the Baseball Hall of Fame.

Rizzuto may be best remembered as the broadcaster of New York Yankee games who exclaimed, "Holy Cow!" every time he witnessed an exciting play.

DENNIS RODMAN

Basketball   Trenton, New Jersey

New Jersey native Dennis Rodman is generally regarded as one of the greatest rebounders in NBA history.

CATHY RUSH

Basketball   West Atlantic City, New Jersey

Cathy Rush coached the Immaculata College women's basketball team to three National Championships before the formation of the NCAA Women's Basketball Tournament.

AL SANTORINI

Baseball   Union, New Jersey

Al Santorini starred in football and baseball at Union High School in New Jersey. Santorini pitched in the major leagues for the Saint Louis Cardinals and the San Diego Padres.

DICK SAVITT

Tennis   Bayonne, New Jersey

In 1957, Dick Savitt won the Wimbledon and Australian tennis titles.

SCOTT SCHOENEWEIS

Baseball   Long Branch, New Jersey

Scott Schoeneweis has pitched for several major-league baseball teams, including the Chicago White Sox and the Anaheim Angels.

L. J. SMITH

Football   Highland Park, New Jersey

L. J. Smith of Rutgers was the third tight end selected in the 2003 NFL draft. He was picked by the Philadelphia Eagles and has been with Eagles for over five seasons.

MICHELE SMITH

Softball   Hunterdon County, New Jersey

Michele Smith was an All-State softball pitcher at Voorhees High School in New Jersey. She has won gold medals as a member of the U.S. Olympic Softball squad and has played professional softball in Japan. Michele also works in sports broadcasting.

MICHAEL STRAHAN

Football   Montclair, New Jersey

Michael Strahan is a star defensive end for the New York Giants and holds the NFL record for quarterback sacks in a season.

JACK TATUM

Football   Passaic, New Jersey

Jack Tatum was an All-American defensive star at Ohio State. Tatum played in the NFL for the Oakland Raiders.

BRIAN TAYLOR

Basketball   Perth Amboy, New Jersey

Brian Taylor left Princeton University early to turn pro and won Rookie of the Year honors in the American Basketball Association (ABA) in 1974. Taylor played for the New York (now New Jersey) Nets and is the brother of NFL star Bruce Taylor.

BRUCE TAYLOR

Football   Perth Amboy, New Jersey

In 1970, Bruce Taylor won Defensive Rookie of the Year honors in the NFL as a member of the San Francisco 49ers.

BOBBY THOMSON

Baseball   Watchung, New Jersey

Bobby Thomson is the man who hit the famous home run known as "the shot heard round the world." His dramatic blast in the ninth inning of the final game of the 1951 play-offs between his New York Giants and the Brooklyn Dodgers earned the Giants the NL pennant. Thomson was also a National League All-Star in 1948, 1949, and 1952.

MARTIN TRUEX JR.

Auto Racing   Mayetta, New Jersey

Martin Truex Jr. is a famous NASCAR driver.

DAVID TYREE

Football   Livington, New Jersey

David Tyree is an NFL wide receiver who played for the Super Bowl champion New York Giants in 2008. He was an NFL Pro Bowl selection in 2005 on special teams.

BILL "BUTCH' VAN BREDA KOLFF

Basketball   Glen Ridge, New Jersey

Butch Van Breda Kolff played in the NBA for several teams, including the New York Knicks. Van Breda Kolff then coached in the National Basketball Association. He also served as the head basketball coach at Princeton University, where he played as an undergraduate.

JEFF VANDERBEEK

Sports Business   Bridgewater, New Jersey

Jeff Vanderbeek is the owner of the New Jersey Devils ice hockey team.

JOHN VAN RYN

Tennis   East Orange, New Jersey

John Van Ryn won six Grand Slam championships as a doubles player.

MO VAUGHN

Baseball   West Orange, New Jersey

Mo Vaughn attended Seton Hall University and was a star baseball player on the Pirates' squad. In the major leagues, Vaughn played for the Anaheim Angels, the Boston Red Sox, and the New York Mets. In 1995, Boston's Mo Vaughn co-led the American League in runs batted in with Albert Belle of the Cleveland Indians. Both players totaled 126 RBIs each that season.

Mo Vaughn–Courtesy S.R.Smith/Seton Hall University Athletics/Sports Media

MICKEY WALKER

Boxing   Elizabeth, New Jersey

Mickey Walker held world welterweight and middleweight titles during the 1920s.

CHARLIE WEIS

Football   Middlesex, New Jersey

Charlie Weis worked as an NFL coach with the New York Jets and the New England Patriots. Weis left the pro ranks to become the head football coach at the University of Notre Dame.

JASON WILLIAMS

Basketball   Plainfield/Metuchen, New Jersey

Jason Williams was an All-American guard at Duke University. He was the second player picked in the 2002 NBA draft. An injury curtailed his professional sports career.

HENRY WITTENBURG

Wrestling   Jersey City, New Jersey

Henry Wittenburg won a gold medal in wrestling in the 192-pound class at the 1948 Olympic Games. He captured a silver medal at the 1952 Olympics.

ROBERT WREN

Tennis   Highland Park, New Jersey

Robert Wren played football, baseball, and tennis at Harvard. Wren was the U.S. National Singles Champion in 1893, 1894, 1896, and 1897. He is a member of the International Tennis Hall of Fame.

AUGUST "ZIMMY" ZIMMERMAN

Cycling   Camden, New Jersey

Zimmy Zimmerman was a professional bike racer in the 1890s. He won races in America, France, Ireland, and Australia.

JEREMY ZUTTAH

Football   Edison, New Jersey

Jeremy Zuttah was a star offensive lineman for the Rutgers football squad that won bowl games in 2007 and 2008. Zuttah was a third- round pick of the Tampa Bay Buccaneers in the 2008 NFL Ddraft.

BIBLIOGRAPHY

Bock, Hal and Ben Olan. *Basketball Stars of 1974* (New York: Pyramid Books, 1974).

Brown, Gene, ed. *New York Times Encyclopedia of Baseball* (Danbury, CT: Grolier Arno Press, 1979).

Connors, Martin, Diane Dupis, and Brad Morgan. *The Olympic Fact Book* (Detroit: Visible Ink Press, 1992).

Davis, Mac. *Giant Book of Sports* (New York: Grosset & Dunlap, 1967).

Durant, John. *The Heavyweight Champions* (New York: Hastings House, 1960).

Gardner, Robert, and Dennis Shortelle. *Forgotten Players—The Story of Black Baseball in America* (New York: Walker & Company, 1993).

Greenspan, Bud. *100 Greatest Moments in Olympic History* (California: General Publishing Group, 1995).

Hickok, Ralph. *Sports Champions* (Boston: Houghton Mifflin, 1995).

Herzog, Brad. *The Sports 100* (New York: MacMillan, 1995).

Hollander, Zander, comp. *Great American Athletes of the 20th Century* (New York: Random House, 1966).

Market, Robert and Nancy Brooks. *For the Record: Women in Sports* (New York: World Almanac Publications, 1985).

Neft, David S., Roland Johnson, Richard Cohen, and Jordan A. Deutsch. *The Sports Encyclopedia: Baseball* (New York: Grosset & Dunlap, 1974).

New York Knicks Media Guide, 2000.

Pellowski, Michael J. *Rutgers Football—A Gridiron Tradition in Scarlet* (New Jersey: Rivergate Books, Rutgers University Press, 2007).

Peterson, Robert. *Only the Ball was White—Negro Baseball* (New Jersey: Prentice-Hall, 1970).

Stockton, J. Roy. *The Gashouse Gang—The Story of the St. Louis Cardinals* (New York: Bantam Books, 1948).

Treat, Roger. *The Encyclopedia of Football* (New Jersey: A.S. Barnes & Company, 1978).

Turkin, Hy, ed. *The Baseball Almanac: 1955* (New York: Cardinal Pocket Book, 1955).

Wallechisky, David. *The Complete Book of the Olympics* (New York: Little, Brown & Co., 1991).

Weston, Stanley. *The Heavyweight Champions* (New York: Ace Publishing, 1970).

ABOUT THE AUTHOR

Michael J. Pellowski was born in New Jersey and grew up in the Garden State to become a star high school baseball and football player. He received a full football scholarship to Rutgers, The State University of New Jersey.

While at Rutgers, Pellowski won seven letters in football and baseball. He was defensive captain of the 1970 Scarlet Knights gridiron squad and won All-East honors. Pellowski still holds the Rutgers record for most quarterback sacks in a game (four versus Lafayette in 1969) and posted a .312 career batting average in baseball.

Mr. Pellowski had professional football trials in the NFL (New England) and CFL (Montreal). He also played semipro football in New Jersey and coached high school football in the Garden State. In addition, he covered high school sports events in New Jersey for cable TV stations and hosted a weekly high school sports talk show seen in the Garden State.

Mr. Pellowski has penned numerous sports books.